On-Line Electrical
Troubleshooting

On-Line Electrical Troubleshooting

Lynn Lundquist

McGraw-Hill Book Company

New York St. Louis San Francisco Auckland
Bogotá Hamburg London Madrid Mexico
Milan Montreal New Delhi Panama
Paris São Paulo Singapore
Sydney Tokyo Toronto

Library of Congress Cataloging-in-Publication Data

Lundquist, Lynn.
  On-line electrical troubleshooting / Lynn Lundquist.

    p. cm.
  Includes index.
  ISBN 0-07-039110-6
  1. Electric testing. I. Title.
TK401.L84 1989
621.31′042—dc19   88-15410
                                                        CIP

1234567890 DOC/DOC 89832109

ISBN 0-07-039110-6

The editors for this book were Harold Crawford and Dennis Gleason,
the designer was Naomi Auerbach, and the production supervisor was
Suzanne W. Babeuf. It was set in Century Schoolbook. It was
composed by the McGraw-Hill Book Company Professional &
Reference Division composition unit.

Printed and bound by R. R. Donnelley and Sons Company.

*For more information about other McGraw-Hill materials,
call 1-800-2-MCGRAW in the United States. In other
countries, call your nearest McGraw-Hill office.*

To my father, Armand Lundquist,
who started me doing electrical work,
and who gave me his moral and spiritual
values for living.

Contents

Preface

I want you to be *excited* with the information you will be learning while reading this book. I believe it is information which will make you a better electrician. However, since I believe learning should be fun, this book has been written so that you can thoroughly enjoy something which will also be of benefit to you in your profession.

The book will teach you how to do truly fast and effective electrical troubleshooting. It will show you how to use state-of-the-art test equipment as well as standard multimeters. The book will also take you beyond wires, relays, and circuits with the goal of encouraging you to become a knowledgeable and innovative electrician.

An author was once asked how long it had taken him to write a book. "My entire lifetime," was his answer. I could agree with that. *On-Line Electrical Troubleshooting* has a much longer history than the nine months I spent actively writing it. It has a longer history than even the two years required to develop the specific technique I am describing. Significantly, the book is the result of others' influence, encouragement, and help. This book is dedicated to my father; his influence has been lifelong in encouraging me in electrical work and in the values he has taught me. I owe a word of thanks to Ray Sytsma, an instructor who has made electrical subjects exciting for many Oregon electricians, including myself. This book was started while I was taking his motor control class.

I would also like to thank a number of individuals representing various companies I have been dealing with. I want each of you to know of my appreciation for your contribution to the completeness of the book. Mr. Robin Miller of Greenlee BEHA Corporation, Peter Sanchez and Roger Seymour of TIF Instruments, Frank Pulice of Hioki-RCC, Edward Grenzic and Kevin Basso of A. W. Sperry Instruments, Justin Harold and Bob Johnson of M. Levin and Son, S. Suzuki and Paul Noesser of Toyomenka America, Jay Stoy of Furnas Electric Company, J. Arnold Nickerson of Nickerson Machinery Co., Edward Juge of Radio Shack, Randy Classen of Brazil Electric Motors, Ron Milstein of Building Tech Bookstore, Paul DuRocher of Vickers, Inc., and Ed Gollon of Amfac Fluid Power.

Two people have helped me with the manuscript. Manuscript work is the tedious and thankless task assigned to unsuspecting friends so that the author can get on with the job. First, thanks go to my wife, Gail (thank you, Honey). Second, special appreciation goes to Mike Hill—a fellow employee—who plowed through the text to see if it made any sense.

Denise Lundquist and Terry Carroll helped me with the photography. Thanks to both of you.

Finally, I appreciate the encouragement of my publisher, Harold Crawford, who believed that it could be done.

Lynn Lundquist

On-Line Electrical Troubleshooting

Getting Started with Electrical Troubleshooting

In this chapter you will be reviewing two major subjects. The first subject is a general introduction to electrical troubleshooting and how it can be of help to you as an electrician. The second subject is safety. For your sake, and for the sake of the equipment you are working on, good safety practices are mandatory for long-term effective troubleshooting.

Introducing Troubleshooting

Think back to your last electrical emergency. Did you make money for your employer by troubleshooting the problem quickly and getting the equipment back into production? (Or better yet, did you diagnose the problem *before* you had a shutdown?) If your answer is "yes," chances of better pay and job advancement are in your favor.

Probably no skill area is more significant in establishing your value as a maintenance electrician than your speed in getting equipment back into production after it has shut down. Even better, if you are able to do your troubleshooting diagnosis and prevent the shutdown altogether (which you may often be able to do after understanding the technique of on-line troubleshooting), your value as an electrician will be greatly enhanced. No single skill will give you more job potential than that of a master troubleshooter. Effective troubleshooting skills should mean greater profitability for your employer and greater job security (and pay) for you.

Now, back to your last electrical emergency. In all likelihood, it took more time to diagnose the cause of the shutdown than it did to fix it. That is typically the case. Because *locating* electrical problems is a major part of machine downtime, this book will attempt to teach you troubleshooting techniques which will reduce the time lost while locating a fault. This will be accomplished by teaching you on-line troubleshooting techniques and by giving you the necessary information and theory with which to do your work. Therefore, the objective of this book is to help you reduce the time it takes you to find an electrical problem in the equipment you are testing.

Defining electrical troubleshooting

Let's take a minute and define our terms. After an electrical problem has caused the complete failure of major equipment, identifying the cause is usually simple. (Admittedly, though, the time required to replace parts may be significant.) Informing management that the entire piece of equipment needs to be replaced is not how I am defining troubleshooting. I am defining troubleshooting as locating a single component failure before extensive damage is done.

The electrician in the next department doesn't understand this definition of troubleshooting. Three days ago—after airing out a compressor room—it was obvious that the motor was "smoked." "That," our electrician friend maintains, "is the simple way to troubleshoot—just look for the burned-out stuff!" Of course, in addition to the motor, other expensive equipment was also replaced: the magnetic contactor, the pressure switch, a timer, and enough miscellaneous items to cause noticeable consternation in the accounting department. However, the electrician didn't mention in the requisition for new equipment that for two days before the motor finally quit, the motor overloads had been continually reset and a sticking bleed valve had been tampered with to keep the compressor running.

Do you see what I mean? Troubleshooting is not explaining why an entire electrical system has been ruined. *Effective troubleshooting will find the first electrical malfunction of any component part on which the normal operation of that electrical system is dependent* (Figure 1.1). By doing that successfully, downtime is reduced, equipment damage is limited, and total repair costs are minimized. And you, the electrician, look good!

A brief discussion of the definition I just gave you is worthwhile. Good troubleshooting usually follows a logical progression:

1. *Good troubleshooting will find the first electrical malfunction of any component part.*   This should be obvious, but in practice it is often violated. Troubleshooting should start at the first indication of an electrical malfunction. It should then begin at the level of finding the first component part which is not operating properly. Too often,

Figure 1.1 Effective troubleshooting is often preventive in nature. Locating a single defective device may prevent expensive future problems. *(A. W. Sperry Instruments, Inc.)*

erratic running is allowed to continue until major electrical damage is done. An example was given of the electrician who finally replaced an entire motor and starting system. If, on the other hand, the first electrical malfunction of a component part had been isolated, nothing more than the faulty bleed valve would have been replaced. Not only would the electrician have saved a great deal of company money if the troubleshooting had been done early, but if the simple on-line troubleshooting procedure (as will be outlined in Chapter 4), had been used, the total troubleshooting time could have been reduced to 15 or 20 minutes. Can you imagine the savings of both time and money that there could have been?

2. *Good troubleshooting will find the first electrical malfunction on which the normal operation of that system is dependent.* Good troubleshooting views a modern electrical installation as a system. Proper maintenance and good troubleshooting must recognize that even the most complex system is dependent on a series of discrete electrical components and devices. A single discrete electrical device such as a compressor bleed valve is as crucial to the overall operation of the compressor system as the 50-hp compressor motor.

Too often, however, the small components are overlooked until the entire system is in jeopardy. On-line troubleshooting, by its very nature, forces you to think about every part of an electrical system in your testing. If you learn to think about the small parts in your testing, I would also hope that as you maintain equipment, you will not become too busy to notice the small, and often inexpensive, electrical items on which your entire system is dependent.

Defining on-line troubleshooting

Before going any further, I need to define on-line troubleshooting. On-line troubleshooting incorporates the two points of good troubleshooting previously mentioned. If you look closely at the first definition, however, you will realize that nothing has been said about the troubleshooting procedure. How is good electrical troubleshooting accomplished?

In Chapter 4 you will be given a complete introduction to the troubleshooting technique I am calling *on-line troubleshooting*. For now, let me give you a very brief explanation so that you understand where you are going as you read the next few chapters.

As you can imagine, there are many different testing procedures which can be used in electrical troubleshooting. Some are done with the electrical power off, and some with the power on. In this book, I am emphasizing a number of procedures where the testing is done on a live circuit—that is the meaning of "on-line" in the title. If you take the necessary safety precautions, there are some advantages to on-line electrical testing; the primary advantage is that you are testing a circuit as it normally operates. (Many times when you turn the power off on a faulty circuit, the problem disappears. You will then spend a great deal of time testing for a problem which no longer exists.)

In on-line troubleshooting you will learn to do a series of tests on a circuit which is energized but is not operating normally. You will learn procedures for isolating the point in that circuit at which some electrical component has failed. You will also be introduced to a number of test instruments which will make your work possible. (If you are familiar at all with electrical testing equipment, you know that standard volt-ohmmeters are not used for resistance measurements with power in the circuit. There are meters presently available, however, which can be used for these kinds of "live" measurements. It is because of these new meters that on-line techniques as I am describing them are possible.)

In on-line troubleshooting you will be testing for continuity on a live circuit. (Continuity means that the circuit is complete.) You will trace the live circuit to the break—or "open" condition—which is causing the circuit to malfunction. At times, you will be doing your testing on both energized and operating circuits.

Looking Ahead

As you read this book, it is my goal that you will become a better troubleshooter. This book is built around a troubleshooting technique which will make you faster in locating electrical problems. You will learn how to do on-line troubleshooting. In some cases, this technique will virtually eliminate machine downtime during the troubleshooting process. It is also my goal to have you understand related non-electrical systems which have a bearing on your effectiveness in solving electrical problems. (This will primarily emphasize a basic understanding of hydraulic systems and hydraulic print reading. There is great value for a maintenance electrician in having the ability to troubleshoot an electrical system on hydraulic equipment. To successfully do that, however, the electrician will need to understand the basic functions of the hydraulic system itself.)

The best way to teach on-line troubleshooting is to stand in front of an electrical panel with a print and show you the steps to take in solving the problem. Since I cannot do that with a book, I will try the next best thing. Throughout you will work with typical electrical malfunctions. You will troubleshoot a plastic injection molding machine using the actual diagrams and realistic electrical problems. (If you know injection molding equipment, it will add interest to the illustrations. However, no prior knowledge is necessary, since the diagrams you will be using are standardized for all industrial equipment.) You will be using a basic ladder diagram which would be similar for any relay-controlled machine.

Reviewing chapters 1 through 8

In the first eight chapters of this book, you will be taught a new electrical troubleshooting technique called on-line troubleshooting. You will begin by studying electrical symbols and diagrams. First, there is a complete explanation of the graphic symbols which are used on a ladder diagram in Chapter 2, Understanding Electrical Symbols. That will be followed in Chapter 3, Understanding Ladder Diagrams, with an explanation of the ladder diagram itself and its code numbers. Then, by starting with actual electrical problems which you would expect to find in your work as a maintenance electrician, you will work toward increasing complexity. Chapter 4, An On-Line Troubleshooting Overview, will give you a broad perspective of this new troubleshooting technique.

In Chapter 5, On-Line Troubleshooting Tools, you will be introduced to some of the new test instruments which are now available to help you do faster troubleshooting. In Chapter 6, Collecting Information, you will be shown how to gather the types of information which will have a bearing on your troubleshooting effectiveness. In Chapter 7, Practical On-Line Troubleshooting, you will be given a complete example of all of the steps necessary when troubleshooting a typical electrical panel circuit. Finally, because multimeters—volt-ohm-meters (VOMs) or digital voltmeters (DVMs)—are so widely used, Chapter 8, Troubleshooting with a Multimeter, will discuss the application of these meters to on-line troubleshooting.

A complete ladder diagram is given in Appendix A. (All of the electrical circuit examples will come from this one diagram.) In order for you to visualize the relationships among the machine's electrical circuits, it will be helpful for you to spend some time looking at the entire diagram.

Once you understand the scope of on-line troubleshooting, you will see many applications for it which are not covered in this text. For the sake of simplicity, this book deals with a limited area of application. I am primarily concerned with equipment having an electrical panel with mechanical relays, timers, hand switches, and the like. The equipment being controlled will have hand switches, buttons, limit switches, and monitor switches (pressure, temperature, etc.). I will not attempt to explain troubleshooting of solid-state controls or programmable controllers. (As a maintenance electrician you will certainly want to familiarize yourself with these controls. However, the theory and practice of troubleshooting these systems are outside the scope of this book.)

Troubleshooting Safety

The importance of safe troubleshooting procedures cannot be stressed enough. Safety for both personnel and equipment must be a high priority in any troubleshooting job. The need for safety does not eliminate well-planned shortcuts or time-saving procedures, but speed cannot become such a dominant goal that prudence is set aside.

The logical place to start in our discussion of safety is the area of working on live circuits. This is particularly true inasmuch as this book is advocating a test procedure which uses live circuits. The admonition to shut everything down before testing has long been stated as an ideal; but I would suggest that for most testing, some live-circuit tests must be done. (The most frequently used test meter in the electrician's toolbox is a voltmeter. Very obviously, this is not a piece of test equipment intended for disconnected circuits! I would therefore draw the conclusion that, in spite of a frequently stated ideal that all testing be done on dead circuits, live-circuit testing is very much a part of the electrician's world.)

The question, then, is not only whether the circuit is live or dead; it is a question of the care taken in using whatever procedure is available. Any troubleshooting procedure is dangerous when safety precautions are ignored. On the other hand, on-line troubleshooting (with a live, or even running, circuit) can be safely done. The real issue is the attention given to safety by the electrician doing the work. (I like the quip I saw in a Navy training manual which said something to the effect that there are old electricians, and there are careless electricians, but there is no such thing as an old, careless electrician.)

As a matter of fact, working on dead circuits can introduce its own hazards from the hands-all-over-everything practice which becomes so deadly if a circuit is accidentally energized. (Recently, an electrician in our city was killed because someone turned on a 480-V circuit to start a welder after the electrician had shut it down for repair. Of course, he should have locked the disconnect in the open position.) There is always the risk of getting sloppy when you think you are working on dead circuits.

You introduce another risk when working on supposedly dead circuits because there are often multiple circuits in the panel. If you are working on the control circuit (usually 120 V or less) it may well be dead; but there can very likely be live 220- or even 480-V controlled circuits running through relays in the same panel which you cannot (or have not!) deenergized. Those isolated, hot circuits have an uncanny way of finding your screwdrivers and pliers—if not you—because you were working as though the entire panel were dead.

After having said what I just did concerning working on live circuits, let me go back and make a major qualification. When you have a choice, kill the power and work on a dead circuit. Some testing will need to be done with the circuit live, but to unnecessarily stick your screwdriver into a hot panel circuit and fiddle with terminal screws or push wires around is asking for trouble. Make it a practice to take the extra time necessary and turn off the power when you have a choice.[1] If there is any possibility of the circuit being energized, use a padlock on the disconnect lockout (Figure 1.2).

I do not believe that on-line troubleshooting introduces any new hazards to electricians. Of necessity, we have all been working on live circuits in most of our troubleshooting procedures for years, though we have been measuring different values than we will be with this

---

[1] I would suggest another caution: *Turn it off yourself.* Never trust anyone else to disconnect the power on something you do not verify before starting work. Poor communication could kill you!

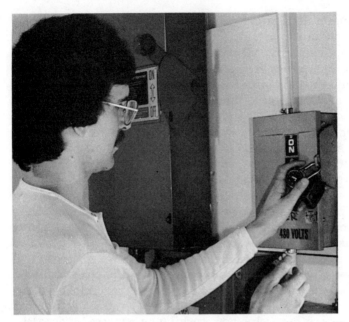

Figure 1.2 Awareness of potential danger and care in working on *all* electrical equipment is the key to true electrical safety. Don't assume that others know where you are working; use lockouts with your personal padlock.

method. The safety requirements, however, have not substantially changed.

General electrical safety precautions

To maintain a high level of electrical safety while you work, there are a number of precautions you should follow. This is, of course, only a start. Your individual job will have its own unique safety requirements. The voltage levels and the types of equipment you are working on—as well as conditions in the plant itself—will introduce conditions which will make demands beyond those given here. However, the following are given as essential basics:

1. *On-line troubleshooting is recommended only for control voltages of 120 V or less.* This is never a technique for higher-voltage circuits, nor is it to be used on motors or any other high-current applications.

2. *Always remember that even with a 120-V control system, you may well have a higher voltage in the panel.* Always work so that you are clear of any of the higher voltages. (Even though you are test-

ing a 120-V system, you are most certainly in close proximity to 240- or 480-V power.)

3. *Avoid unnecessary exposure to potential shock.* Use your meter carefully when you are touching exposed current carrying terminals. Don't move wires to gain better access when the power is on. Above all, *shut the power off before starting any required repair work.*

4. *When working in a live panel, make it a practice to avoid leaning on or touching grounded areas.* (In other words, don't lean against the panel or hold on to the door while you are checking circuits.)

5. *Use all test equipment safely and according to the manufacturer's recommendations.* Do not use it for higher voltages or in testing conditions for which it was not designed. If it is not an autoranging meter, always start on high settings so that you get a low scale reading on your initial test; this will protect you and the meter in case the voltage (or amperage) is higher than anticipated.

6. *Use good housekeeping procedures inside a panel.* Keep tools, wire spools, and all of the other odds and ends you are working with outside the panel when they are not in use. The inside of the panel is not a workbench—*Keep it clear!*

7. *Use good electrical practices even in temporary wiring for testing.* You may at times need to make alternate connections, but make them secure enough so that they are not in themselves an electrical hazard.

8. *If you are planning on working on a circuit as though it were dead, make certain that it is truly dead.* Presumption at this point can kill you. It is a good practice to take a meter reading before starting work on a "dead" circuit. (It is also a good practice to confirm the meter before relying on it. I know an electrician who is working in a large port facility where radio communication is used to keep in touch with field personnel. Radio transmissions can trip the internal circuit breakers in the electricians' voltmeters. The port has a potentially hazardous situation where an electrician may take a voltage reading and assume a circuit is dead, when in fact the meter is not functioning because a radio transmission made in close proximity tripped the internal circuit breaker.)

For all of the lists that could be made for safety practices, however, there is a single admonition which will produce the safest working conditions. *Use good judgment.* You the electrician should have the best understanding of what the particular job you are doing entails. With that as a background, and with a proper understanding of the inherent hazards in electrical work, you should then be able to decide what is, and what is not, acceptable safety practice as you proceed.

Profitable Troubleshooting

Are you ready for the promise? If you master the simple technique of on-line troubleshooting as you will see it developed in this book, you will seldom spend more than 15 or 20 minutes isolating an electrical malfunction in a relay or contact-actuated piece of equipment. What is more, you will be able to do the entire job—up to the final confirmation of the faulty component—from the electrical panel. You will not be testing individual components and switches at their location. You will learn how to take almost all of the readings from inside of the panel to the point that you can isolate faulty switches or electrical devices (solenoids, etc.) from the terminal board of the panel.

Of course, I am assuming that you have a basic understanding of the equipment you are troubleshooting.[2] I am also assuming that you will have a complete ladder diagram of the equipment. (In Chapter 10 you will learn how to circumvent the ladder diagram if it is not available, though needless to say, the ladder diagram will be one of your most important tools.) It should also be obvious that to be of the greatest usefulness, the machine should be represented by an up-to-date ladder diagram. (But be prepared. You will open the panel some day to be greeted by the magnificent rewiring work of an "old timer" who left jumper wires in the panel like spider webs and failed to make a single notation of any of the changes on the wiring diagram!) I am also assuming that all of the wires are properly marked (with wire numbers) in accordance with the ladder diagram notations. (In Chapter 10 you will also learn how to identify a wire which has lost its number.)

Finally, to make my promise come true, I am assuming that you will have the appropriate test equipment to do the job. There will be a complete description of the equipment you will need for on-line troubleshooting in Chapter 5, On-Line Troubleshooting Tools. Chapter 8, Troubleshooting with a Multimeter, and Chapter 9, Specialized Tests and Equipment, will introduce additional equipment and testing procedures which will help you do a better and faster job. What you need will be neither excessively expensive nor complicated to use, but to do your testing at the speed I am suggesting, you will need to test for continuity with the control circuit energized.

---

[2] Maybe you were called in to work on something you've never seen before. So in Chapter 6 I'll tell you how to get the operator to give you the information you will need to do your troubleshooting.

Beyond On-Line Troubleshooting

In the final chapters of the book, I want to go beyond the technique described as on-line troubleshooting. In each of these chapters, effectiveness in troubleshooting—which results in greater troubleshooting speed—is the underlying goal. In Chapter 9 you will be shown some specific testing procedures with selected testing equipment such as clamp-on ammeters and megohmmeters. Chapter 10, Expanding On-Line Troubleshooting Applications, will show you how to take the basic on-line troubleshooting procedures and apply them to other types of electrical circuits. There will also be a section describing the testing procedures when an electrical diagram is not available.

The final two chapters go beyond applied electrical troubleshooting. In Chapter 11, Broadening the Electrician's Horizons, you are encouraged to broaden your knowledge beyond mere electrical skills; your troubleshooting effectiveness will often be a result of your awareness of nonelectrical information. Finally, in Chapter 12, Troubleshooting Hydraulic Systems, you will be shown how to read basic hydraulic prints and use the information for troubleshooting electrically operated hydraulic systems.

Chapter Review

A primary goal of any maintenance electrician should be greater production time from plant equipment. Thus, the greater the electrician's speed in performing troubleshooting tasks, the less the downtime that will be accumulated on the equipment. The value of the maintenance electrician, then, is directly proportional to his or her troubleshooting speed and ability to get equipment back into operation.

A proper definition of electrical troubleshooting states that it is the process of finding the first electrical malfunction of any component part on which the normal operation of that electrical system is dependent. In both troubleshooting and plant maintenance, industrial electrical equipment is viewed as a complete system.

Electrical safety must be uppermost in every electrician's mind. Whether the work being done is installation, maintenance, or troubleshooting, the most important safety consideration is the care and judgment used while working with electrical equipment. This is particularly true when working in close proximity to other circuits of a higher voltage. Poor judgment, sloppy working procedures, and high-risk short cuts are an invitation to personal injury and equipment damage. Each set of working conditions will have its own safety criteria which extend beyond this chapter's generalized safety procedures.

Chapter Questions

Thinking through the text

1. In contrast to the practice of replacing entire systems because there has been a major shutdown, when (and where) should good troubleshooting start?

2. Why is it important that you be aware of the maintenance and trouble-shooting of individual electrical devices and components in a system's circuit?

3. What is the difference between on-line and off-line (or dead-circuit) testing?

4. Questioning whether the circuit is live or dead is not the only criterion for safety. What is the greatest concern in maintaining electrical troubleshooting safety?

5. What caution is given concerning multiple circuits in a panel?

6. Summarize each of the eight safety precautions given in the first chapter.

Deepening your electrical understanding

7. If you work in an industrial or production plant, try to compute your value to the company when you reduce machine downtime. If it is available to you, obtain the dollar-per-hour machine rate for something you are likely to troubleshoot. Divide that figure by 60 (minutes) and you will have the machine cost per minute. (If you cannot get these figures you will need to do some skill-ful guessing.) In addition, you will need to figure other costs such as wasted material, idle employee time, etc. Try to assign a realistic dollar figure for each minute of that machine's downtime. As an example, how much would you save the company if you were able to reduce your troubleshooting time from 2 hours to 15 minutes for a given breakdown? (Repair time is additional but the same for either example.)

8. From your answer to the previous question, you should be able to see the value gained by improving your troubleshooting skills. Many times, however, good speed is as much a function of how you schedule your work as it is a matter of good troubleshooting. Give some examples of how good scheduling (of either your work in troubleshooting per se or of equipment and production scheduling in the plant) can reduce downtime cost.

2

Understanding
Electrical Symbols

*In this chapter you will be learning the meanings
of the graphic and numerical information used on
typical electrical diagrams. In the first section, you
will study the electrical symbols most frequently
used on industrial electrical diagrams. (These
diagrams are generally in the form of ladder
diagrams). In the second section, you will study the
numerical coding systems used on these same
diagrams.*

Electrical Symbols

Table 2.1 shows the electrical symbols which you are most likely to
encounter in industrial maintenance electrical work. Since you need
to be familiar with all of these symbols and their functions, it will be
helpful for you to stop and carefully look through the table. (No specific explanation will be given in this chapter for feeder circuit, disconnect, circuit breaker, or overload symbols. However, it is important
that you understand the functions and schematic representation of
each one of these symbols. The purpose of this chapter is to acquaint
you with the circuit symbols you will use after establishing that there
is power to the circuits you are testing.)

Since the focus of this book is electrical troubleshooting with the use
of a ladder diagram, there are only a limited number of symbols which
you will need to know from memory. These are shown in Table 2.2.
Review this table, taking the time necessary to understand each symbol that is new to you.

As you study the symbols, you will realize that there is a simple
logic in the graphic representations. Lines are drawn to represent
current-carrying paths, dots and circles are used to represent points

TABLE 2.1 Standard Electrical Wiring Diagram Symbols

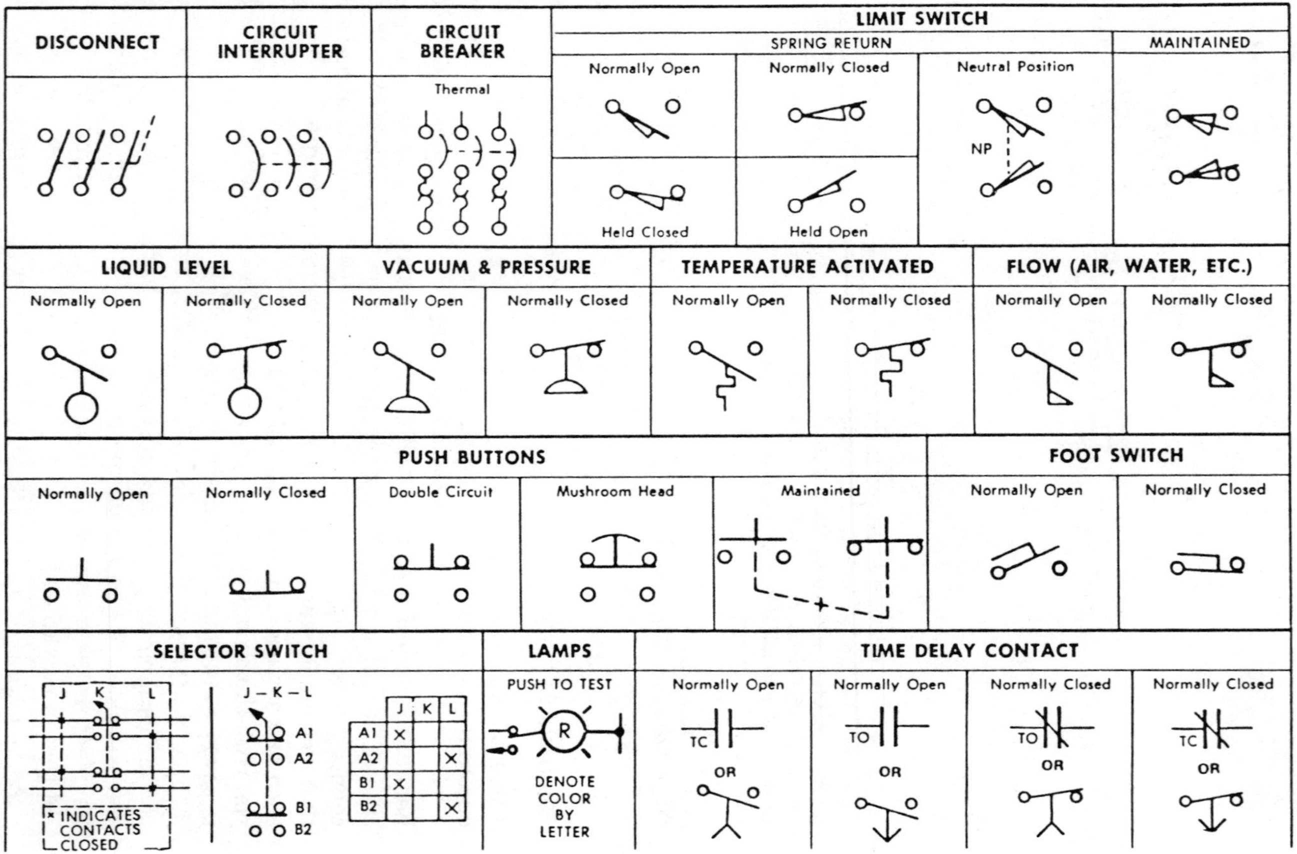

GENERAL CONTACTS		CONDUCTORS		MAGNET COILS		CONTROL TRANSFORMER	METER
Normally Open	Normally Closed	Not Connected	Connected	Shunt	Series	H1 H3 H2 H4 X2 X1	VM AM

GROUND	FULL WAVE RECTIFIER	HORN, SIREN	BELL, BUZZER	MOTOR	OVERLOAD RELAY	FUSE
	AC DC AC DC			3 Phase / MOTOR	Thermal	

AUTO TRANSFORMER	RESISTOR		CONNECTIONS	BATTERY
	Adjustable / RES	Fixed / RES	Mechanical / Mechanical Interlock	

SOURCE: Courtesy of Furnas Electric Company.

TABLE 2.2   Symbols Most Frequently Used in Troubleshooting

SOURCE: Courtesy of Furnas Electric Company.

where a conductor can be "touched" to make an electrical contact, switches are drawn so that you can mentally "close" or "open" them, and so on. The following explanations should help you understand the information in Tables 2.1 and 2.2.

Conductors.   A conductor is a line through which current can flow. Conductors may cross each other but make no electrical contact; this is represented by intersecting lines with no dot. On the other hand, the conductors may make contact (that is, they are common); this is represented by a heavy dot at the junction.

There is another symbol which is infrequently used for intersecting conductors. You should be familiar with it because you may see it on older diagrams. The common conductors are represented by intersecting lines, but no heavy dot is used. The conductors which cross each other but make no electrical contact are represented by horseshoe loops around the junction point. The loop is the key to identifying which of the two systems is being used. If there are no loops where the conductors cross, then the diagram follows current usage. If there are loops at any conductor crossings, then the diagram is older, and all crossed conductors are read as common even though there is no dot at the intersection.

If you look at the ladder diagram in Appendix A, you will notice that it is a hybrid. Common crossing conductors are indicated with a dot. On the other hand, conductors which are not common but which cross are looped. For an example of looped conductors, look at the left-hand side of the diagram on lines 18, 29, and 36.

On some diagrams you will see both heavy and light conductor lines. The heavy lines are used for high-current-carrying conductors. (That is, the main lines that are controlled by the high-current electrical devices in the panel, including the motor leads, the main disconnects and thermals, etc.) The lighter lines are used for the control circuit (lower-voltage control panel circuits such as switches, timers, and relays.)

Switches.   Notice that a switch always has two small circles on the end of the conductor. Touching something across the two circles closes an electrical "bridge" between the two conductors. You will also notice that the diagram shows some of the switches as open (the line representing the switch is not touching at least one of the circles) and some of the switches as closed (the switch line is touching both circles). This brings us to another important area of switch terminology. Switches are always designated as being either normally open (NO) or normally closed (NC). A normally open switch in its relaxed or normal state is nonconductive. A normally closed switch is the opposite and carries a current in its relaxed state.

You will also notice that the diagram shows some of the switches as *open* (the line representing the switch is not touching at least one of the circles) and some as *closed* (the switch line is touching both circles). *The diagram always represents switches and contacts in the "off" or relaxed position.* For example, Figure 2.1 shows the motor start circuit. PBS (push-button stop) on line 7 is open until it is pushed. On the other hand, PBM (push-button motor start) is closed until it is pushed. Line 4 shows a door safety limit switch (LS10) which is open unless the door is latched shut. (An "open" door is considered to be in the relaxed position.) On line 8 there are two relay contacts (cr1), both controlled by relay 1. The position of the relay contacts is shown as if the power were off. In other words, with the power off, the relay contact between wire 2 and wire 88 is closed. (The slash indicates normally closed contacts.) On the other hand, with the power still off, the relay contact between wire 2 and wire 4 is open.

The diagram also shows how a limit switch will actually function when it is cycled. On line 16 in Figure 2.2 two limit switches are shown. Notice that the limit switch is always drawn so that there is a "ramp," or the base of an inverted right triangle, facing the left-hand side of the diagram. You can visualize a roller moving along the ramp. If the roller is moved to the right, the switch contact arm is moved down. If the roller is moved to the left, the contact arm returns to the up position. (The contact arm is spring-loaded—it always wants to move to the up position.) Look carefully at limit switch 1 (LS1) and you will notice that the contact arm is drawn above the contact circle

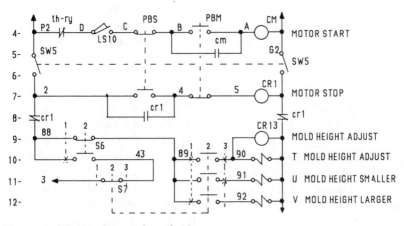

Figure 2.1 Diagram lines 4 through 12.

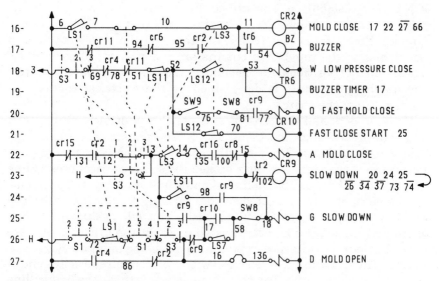

Figure 2.2   Diagram lines 16 through 27.

on the end of wire 7. From that schematic representation, you can tell that LS1 (or that function if the limit switch had more than one circuit) is a normally open (NO) switch which is closed when it is activated. On the other hand, limit switch 3 (LS3) on the same line is drawn showing the contact arm under the contact circle on the end of wire 11. Thus, you can tell that LS3 is a normally closed (NC) limit switch and will open when it is activated.

A single switch may have multiple circuits. Lines 10, 11, and 12 show four circuits contained in switch S7. (Refer back to Figure 2.1.) The first circuit is common to wires 3 and 43. The second circuit is common to wires 89 and 90. The third circuit is common to wires 89 and 91. The final circuit is common to wires 89 and 92. A single switch may be used to control any number of circuits; switch S7, for example, controls four circuits. In the case of switch S7, three circuits are common to wire 89. This is not always the case, however, because circuits controlled by a switch may be completely isolated. Figure 2.2 shows limit switch LS1 on lines 16 and 26. These two circuits are entirely separate. (If you look at the complete diagram in Appendix A, you will see a third circuit for limit switch LS1 on line 46.) Other types of switches may also have multiple circuits. Figure 2.1 shows a toggle switch (SW5) on lines 5 and 6 with two circuits. Multiple circuits are often used in push-button switches, selector switches, etc.

Do not confuse the terms "position" and "circuit" when referring to a switch or push button. You will be studying selector switch S7 in the next several paragraphs. You have just seen that switch S7 has four circuits. You will also see that it has three positions. The number of positions and the number of circuits are independent of each other. The number of positions is a mechanical function built into the switch; the number of circuits is determined by the electrical connections made through the switch.

If you understand the concept of a switch's multiple circuits, then you will understand the meaning of the connecting broken line. Again, look at Figure 2.1. You will see five different switches or push buttons that are connected with broken lines. The vertical broken line between push button PBS on lines 4 and 7 indicates that the push button is mechanically connected so that pushing the button will move both contacting elements simultaneously. You will be studying switch S7 in just a moment. However, as you look at the drawing, you see that the four circuits are represented as being mechanically connected. Thus, moving the selector switch will simultaneously control each of the four circuits. The point being made is this—the broken line indicates a mechanical function. *It is not an electrical conductor.* Do not make the mistake of reading a broken line as a part of the electrical circuit.

Selector switches are the most difficult to visualize. Switch S7 on line 11 (refer back to Figure 2.1), which is diagrammatically connected (represented by the broken line) to lines 10, 11, and 12, is a single switch. It has three positions as indicated by the numbers 1, 2, and 3 above it. The broken line passes through the second position indicator. Thus, as indicated in the drawing, the contacts are either open or closed in the second position. For the other two positions (positions 1 and 3), the asterisk indicates when contacts are closed.[1] (On line 11, the single asterisk for position 3—adjacent to wire 91—indicates that wires 89 and 91 are closed when the switch is in position 3. However, they are not closed when the switch is in position 1 because there is no asterisk. You also know that it is not closed in position 2 because the drawing shows it as open. However, on line 10, the asterisks on both positions 1 and 3 indicate that the circuit is closed in positions 1 and 3 and the drawing indicates that it is open in position 2.) Thus, the diagram shows which of the contacts are open or closed for each of the three positions. This switch also has four circuits. It controls a circuit between wires 3 and 43, and three circuits between

---

[1] You will occasionally see another form which uses X to indicated closed, and O to indicate open. Thus, line 10 would be indicated as XOX, line 11 would be indicated as OOX, and line 12 would be indicated as XOO.

TABLE 2.3   Switch Position Table

	Closed	Open
Position 1	89-90 / 89-92	3-43 / 89-91
Position 2	3-43	all others
Position 3	89-90 / 89-91	3-43 / 89-92

wires 89 and 90, 91, and 92. Table 2.3 shows in table form the information which is given by the asterisks and numbers on the ladder diagram for the three-position switch S7.

Switch symbols include a number of specialized switches for sensing pressure, temperature, flow, etc. Your need to know these symbols will primarily be dependent on your particular application. Do notice, however, the way in which they are schematically represented; the symbol designates whether they are normally open (NO) or normally closed (NC).

Push buttons. Push buttons are shown as an upside down T. The leg of the T is the thumb button, and the cross of the T is the electrical contact. If the electrical contact line is above the contact circles shown on the ends of the connecting wires, there will be a space between the circles and the line. This schematic representation indicates that the contact is open until it is pushed. If the electrical contact line is below the circles, the line will touch the circles. This second representation indicates that the push button is closed until it is pushed. Push buttons are always shown as being spring-loaded so that the button will return to an "up" (top-of-page) position. (Look back at the two push buttons on line 7 in Figure 2.1 for examples of a normally open and a normally closed push button.)

A push-button switch, control switch, or limit switch may have multiple contacts. Rather than physically grouping all of a given button's or switch's functions together, the mechanical interconnection is represented by a broken line. Lines 4 and 7 (Figure 2.1) show two push buttons each. There are only two actual buttons (not four); each push button has two functions. The broken line between them shows that they are the same button. In the case of the push buttons on lines 4 and 7, the buttons are physically arranged on the diagram so that they are horizontally aligned. That may not always be the case, as two functions of a single switch may be widely separated on the ladder diagram. Notice the limit switch LS11 on lines 18 and 24. (Refer back to Figure 2.2.) That single limit switch also controls two functions. (That is, the limit switch has two sets of contacts within the single switch body which are isolated from each other.) The two widely separated functions are shown as being housed within a single switch body by the broken line connecting them.

Contacts. Contacts are generally divided into two broad categories: instantly operating contacts and timed contacts. Instantly operating contacts (generally relay or timer contacts) are indicated by two parallel lines($\dashv\vdash$). Normally open (NO) contacts are drawn as shown above. Normally closed (NC) contacts have a slash through them ($\dashv\!\!\!/\!\!\vdash$). Timed contacts are generally those in which some sort of device delays the making (or breaking) of the contact after the initiation point. (Until recently, timed contacts were generally pneumatic or oil-filled dashpot units. These units used a moving piston in an air- or oil-filled cylinder to delay the switching action. In newer electrical panels, you will see more solid-state timers. These timers may be either fixed, i.e., having a preset time interval, or variable.) As in all other symbols, contacts are indicated as though they are in the deenergized state.

Coils. Table 2.2 shows two symbols which need further clarification. These two symbols are always found on the right-hand side of the diagram. The symbol drawn as a circle is called a shunt coil. In most cases, you can think of the shunt coil as a low-power device (a relay, a timer, or a counter) which is controlling a higher-power device (such as a solenoid). The shunt coil may also be an indicator (such as a panel light). The sawtooth symbol is called a series coil. The series coil is usually a higher-power device and is the final electrical control device in that circuit. (In the circuit you are studying, the series coils are all hydraulic or air solenoid valves.)

Phantom circuits. There is a final explanation that should be given. Referring to Figure 2.3, you will see a small circuit on line 39 and line 40 that has no physical connection with any other part of the circuit. This particular diagram is showing a trigger circuit for the counter; it is connected to the counter terminals 4 and 5, but it is not a current-carrying circuit. (A trigger circuit merely "makes-and-breaks" across two terminals of the counter or timer to initiate the counting or timing process.) The complete counter is not shown on the diagram; only its functions are shown. This simplifies the diagram by avoiding the complexity of adding the complete counter schematic. The single function you need to identify is drawn with no actual connections shown; you see only the wire and terminal markings.

Because any given electrical diagram represents a specialized piece of equipment, there will be information on the drawing which is

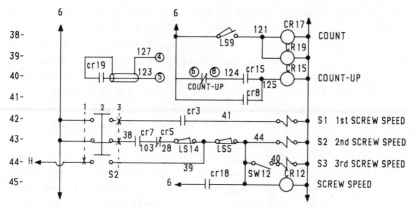

Figure 2.3   Diagram lines 38 through 45.

unique to that electrical circuit. This information is usually self-explanatory and can be understood with a little patience. The information will often be given as supplementary diagrams in the main drawing's margin.

Diagram Numbering Systems

The ladder diagram will use numbers (and letters) to help you locate electrical devices, numbered wire locations, and schematic locations. The following categories are the primary code systems you will need to understand.

Line numbers.   On the left-hand side of the ladder diagram you will find a series of consecutive numbers from 1 at the top to whatever number of lines are included in the diagram on the bottom. (The diagram you are using terminates with line 84 at the bottom. Refer to the complete ladder diagram in Appendix A.) These numbers merely identify the lines on the physical drawing; you will not find these numbers anywhere in the electrical panel. These numbers are only used as an aid in reading the diagram.

Wire numbers.   You will find a number (or letter) on the end of each wire throughout the entire machine. These numbers correspond to the wire identification numbers on the ladder diagram. Thus, on line 7 (Figure 2.1) you will see three wire numbers: 2, 4, and 5. If you were to open the control panel of the machine and look at either of the two push buttons or the relay shown on the diagram as being connected by wire 4, you would find wires with number 4 identifying bands on their ends. The diagram shows these lines intersecting as a T. In fact, you will find four wire ends with number 4; one end will be on relay contact cr1 from line 8. Then, there are two push buttons which have a number 4 wire. One of these push buttons will have one number 4 wire, while the other push button terminal will be used to join two number 4 wires. (You would never expect to see a midwire splice on a control wire as assembled by the manufacturer.) On the other hand, wire 5 will only have two numbered ends; one on push button PBM, and the other on CR1's relay coil.

(There is an exception to the number of wire ends you would expect to find. Wires from the machine will be bundled and brought to an electrical panel—usually in one or more flexible, liquid-tight conduits. Close to the entrance area in the panel, you will find a long terminal block. The incoming wires will terminate on the terminal block with the control panel wires of the same wire number also running to the terminal block. Each junction point of the terminal block will have a wire number marker on it. Generally, the ladder diagram gives no indication of this terminal block. However, you will find this terminal block to be an invaluable aid in troubleshooting.)

Wires common to each other are usually designated by a single number on the diagram. For example, wire 2 (lines 6, 7, and 8 shown in Figure 2.1) has a single number designation. Yet you know that all of the wires common to this numbered wire are also number 2 wires.

Notice that on line 45 (Figure 2.3) there is a 6 and an arrow (6←). This notation indicates an imaginary line drawn from the arrow to the wire number indicated. This separated circuit designation prevents complicated and confusing lines. It means that wire 6 from line 45 is connected to wire 6 on the left side of the diagram (which runs vertically from line 15 to line 46).[2]

Output device and component numbers (or letters). Each ladder diagram will designate output devices and components[3] in the diagram with code letters and numbers. In the diagram you are using, relays are designated as CR1, CR2, and so forth. (CR is electrical shorthand for

---

[2] Wire numbers and terminal numbers are separate designations. It is only by coincidence that wire 6 and terminal 6 are common.

[3] The terms "output device" and "component" need to be defined. As I am using the terms in this book, component is the more general term. It will include switches, buttons, or generalized current-carrying parts. It may also be used as a general descriptive term for any part in the electrical circuit, thus avoiding the complexity of naming both output devices and components. Output devices, however, are specifically defined as shunt or series parts of the circuit as found on the right side of the ladder diagram. An output device is always the final part of the individual circuit, and is the controlled point of the circuit.

control relay. You will also notice that there are CR designations in both upper- and lowercase letters. The uppercase designation indicates the relay coil circuit. The lowercase letters indicate a set of contacts on that relay. Thus, CR1 in the diagram is the solenoid coil. On the other hand, there will be a number of contacts on this same relay which will be designated as cr1 throughout the diagram.) Electrically operated hydraulic solenoids are designated on this diagram with letters as A, B, etc. (Thus A is the electrical solenoid pilot coil which activates the hydraulic circuit which closes the mold.) Timers are designated as TR1, TR2, etc. (Again, as in the case of relays, there is a distinction made between the timer motor or solid-state timer circuit and the timer contacts. The timer motor is designated with uppercase letters, e.g., TR1, and the internal timer contacts with lowercase letters, e.g., tr1.)

Limit switches, selector switches, etc., generally have a number and legend on the side that describes the function of the switch. (Thus, in Figure 2.1, limit switch 10 on line 4 is designated as LS10. On the legend section of the diagram, you will find a listing of all the limit switches, where you find LS10 designated as the "rear gate safety." Were you to go to the rear gate on the machine and physically locate this limit switch, there would actually be an identification label on the switch itself with the designation LS10.)

Relay contact numbers. Throughout the diagram, relay and other controlled contact locations are designated by number and symbol on the circuit line they are controlling. For example, on line 22 (Figure 2.2) you will find that there are four relay contacts which must be in the closed position in order for the circuit to operate. These are designated with their respective relay numbers, cr15, cr2, cr16, and cr8. If you physically located each of these relays, you would find the wire numbers as given on the ladder diagram on their terminal blocks.

Terminal numbers. In some cases, the actual terminal of an electrical device is designated. This is often the case with timers or counters, since the terminals on these devices have specialized functions. (Connecting line voltage to an inappropriate terminal may destroy a timer.) Lines 39 and 40 in Figure 2.3 give four examples of this type of designation. The counter (identified on the drawing as "count-up") has an eight-pin base. The actual base in the electrical panel has embossed terminal numbers. These terminal numbers correspond with a number in a circle on the ladder diagram. Thus, by looking at the diagram, you know that wire 127 goes to terminal 4 on the counter. Similarly, wire 123 goes to terminal 5, wire 6 goes to terminal 6, and wire 124 goes to terminal 8.

Location numbers. On the right side of the ladder diagram next to the common control wire is a series of descriptions and numbers. The descriptions tell us the function of that circuit by the output device it controls. (Line 16 shown in Figure 2.2 controls relay CR2. Relay CR2 is identified as "mold close.") To the right of the identifying description is a series of numbers. In this case, the numbers at the extreme right of line 16 are 17, 22, $\overline{27}$, and 66. These are diagram line numbers (not wire numbers) where you will find contacts controlled by this relay. In other words, if you look on diagram line 17 (Figure 2.2), you will find a set of contact points designated cr2. Similarly, lines 22, 27, and 66 will also have cr2 contact points. Notice the line drawn over 27 ($\overline{27}$). The overbar indicates that the points are normally closed. Look at cr2 on line 27 (Figure 2.2); the points have a slash, indicating that they are, in fact, normally closed.

Chapter Review

Electrical symbols and diagram formats have been standardized in an attempt to simplify reading electrical prints. With little exception, if you are familiar with the symbols in Table 2.1, you will be able to read almost any industrial electrical diagram.

Electrical symbols are a graphic representation of electrical circuit logic. Conductors (and conducting elements in switches, relays, etc.) are represented by lines. Controlled parts of the circuit (relays, switches, push buttons, timers, etc.) are represented by graphic symbols which will complete an open part of the circuit. The diagram always represents switches and contacts in the off or relaxed position.

The complete ladder diagram uses number (and letter) codes to designate specialized information. Line numbers (on the extreme left of the diagram) are solely for the purpose of diagram referencing. Wire numbers are markings on both the diagram and the wire itself which identify individual conductors. Each common conductor has a unique wire number. Component and output device numbers are used to identify the physical parts of the electric circuit. Uppercase letters (with numbers) identify the electrically activated coil or motor of the component. Lowercase letters (with numbers) indicate the controlled contacts of that same component. Other number codes include terminal numbers, which are used to indicate the appropriate terminal location for a given wire, and location numbers on the right side of the ladder diagram, which are used to indicate the location of the contacts controlled by that component.

Chapter Questions

Thinking through the text

1. Describe the electrical function of each of the symbols shown in Table 2.2.

2. All make-and-break devices (switches, contacts points, push buttons, etc.) are represented in a given operating position. What is that position? In what operating position are the switches for mechanical units (doors, motion controls, etc.) represented?

3. What do the letter designations NO and NC stand for? Explain their meanings.

4. Draw the symbols for shunt and series coils. Explain their differences.

5. Electrical components with contacts (such as relays and timers) are referred to with both upper- and lowercase letters. What do uppercase letters designate? Lowercase letters?

6. Explain the meaning of the location numbers and the overbars (lines) above the location numbers which are listed on the right-hand side of the ladder diagram.

Deepening your electrical understanding

7. Draw a three-position, three-circuit selector switch. (You do not need to show the switch as being connected to any circuit.) Show one circuit in the open position and two circuits in the closed position. Use asterisks and broken lines to indicated the switch's switching pattern. Represent the switching function by a table showing each of the three switch positions.

8. Draw a circuit using at least six of the symbols shown in the chapter. Explain the circuit's function and the purpose of the individual circuit components represented by the symbols.

9. Electrical symbols are often a graphic representation of what is taking place electrically (and mechanically). Draw four electrical symbols and explain the symbolic logic represented by each.

Understanding
Ladder Diagrams

*In this chapter you will learn to understand an
electrical system's functions by visualizing the
relationship of individual electrical components
(represented by symbols) to the entire electrical
circuit. An electrical circuit is drawn as either a
ladder diagram or a wire diagram. This chapter
will help you to understand the relationship
between electrical symbols and the ladder diagram.
A brief explanation of wire diagrams will also be
given at the end of the chapter.*

Introducing the Ladder Diagram

A ladder (or line[1]) diagram is a schematic representation of an electrical circuit. It is drawn in an H format, with the energized power
conductors represented by vertical lines and the individual circuits
represented by horizontal lines. (If you are not familiar with the layout of a ladder diagram, refer to Appendix A.) Notice that the ladder
diagram is defined as a schematic representation of the circuit; it is
not a physical representation. The electrical components and conductors are arranged according to their electrical function in the circuit,
that is, schematically. (The wire diagram—which will be discussed
briefly at the end of the chapter—is a physical representation. In
other words, the electrical components and conductors are arranged
on the basis of their actual physical relationship to each other.)

Simplicity is the purpose of the schematic layout of the ladder diagram. Diagram complexity is greatly reduced by indicating each cir-

---

[1] The terms "ladder diagram" and "line diagram" can be used interchangeably. In
this book, the term "ladder diagram" will be used.

cuit as a single vertical line. (Compare Figures 3.1 and 3.3. Although these two diagrams are for different circuits, notice the larger number of lines used in Figure 3.3 to represent functions similar to those shown in Figure 3.1.) Thus, by its vertical arrangement, the ladder diagram can be used to represent very large electrical circuits by merely increasing the length of the circuit diagram. This does not add to the difficulty of reading individual circuit lines. As a matter of fact, when you fully understand the ladder diagram, you will appreciate its genius for reducing a complex electrical circuit to an extremely manageable graphic representation.

The ladder diagram is a logical circuit representation

Using the ladder diagram will be relatively simple now that you understand the meaning of the electrical symbols. The ladder diagram merely represents the current paths (shown as the rungs of the ladder) to each of the controlled or energized output devices, that is, the relays, solenoids, timers, and whatever else is electrically controlled and causes the equipment to operate). As you read from left to right along a ladder diagram line, you will see each of the switches and contacts (the electrical components) that control the electrical current to the output device.

The motor-starting circuit is a good one to start with, both because it is relatively uncomplicated, and because you are already familiar with it from the previous chapter. Figure 3.1 shows diagram lines 4 and 5. This is the current path needed to energize and lock the motor's magnetic starter (which is designated as CM). For the magnetic

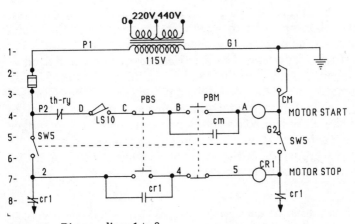

Figure 3.1   Diagram lines 1 to 8.

starter (CM) to cycle, wire P2 must be energized and a series of electrical contacts must close. The ladder diagram shows each of the contacts through which the circuit for a given electrical component output device must pass. As you read from left to right along line 4, you see that the circuit will pass through four individual contacts: the motor overload circuit (th-ry), the rear gate safety (LS10), the motor stop push button (PBS), and the motor start push button (PBM). In fact, the electrical current will follow exactly the same path as shown on line 4 to reach the motor's magnetic starter coil (CM). This is the purpose of the ladder diagram—each line is a graphic representation of the current path for a given electrical component or output device in the actual electrical panel.

You should be able to immediately see the value of the ladder diagram as a troubleshooting aid. As you will see later in the troubleshooting section, this diagram will allow you to follow the path of the circuit until you find the one electrical component or output device that is failing to function. Since the ladder diagram is an exact representation of that current path, you can do various voltage or continuity checks along the path to verify the operation (or failure) of each of the components or their wire connections.

The ladder diagram only represents electrical functions

You must remember, however, that the ladder diagram represents the equipment's electrical functions; it does not represent the physical wiring layout of the machine. You will see sections of the panel wiring where the physical locations of various components are adjacent to each other and are connected by a single wire just as it is indicated in the diagram. However, the wiring layout in terms of the physical location of components is often quite different from the ladder diagram representation. This is true simply because switches and buttons are often in quite widely separated locations on the actual machine.

You have already seen that the number of lines used on the drawing are kept to a minimum. An example of the reduction of lines is the indication of a common point by a heavy dot and intersecting lines. (For an example of a midwire connection on the diagram, look at wire 4 on line 7 in Figure 3.1.) In fact, this is not how you will find the wiring physically arranged in the machine. Wires always terminate on electrical component terminals. Wires are joined on terminal lugs—never at a midwire point. You would also expect to see electrical components widely separated on the actual machine, although they are represented on the diagram as being adjacent to each other. With these basic qualifications concerning the physical arrangement of the circuit, however, you will find the ladder diagram to be a great help in electrical troubleshooting.

Reading the Ladder Diagram

For you to effectively use the ladder diagram, there are some relatively simple points that you will need to understand concerning the physical representation of the diagram symbols.

Vertical diagram lines

On the right side of the diagram, there is always a common grounded conductor represented by a vertical line. (In Figure 3.1, this is the line on the controlled side of switch SW5 which connects with wire G2. If you look at the complete diagram in Appendix A, you will see that this wire runs to the bottom of the diagram.) The common grounded conductor will be identified by either a number (which would be used on both the diagram and on all of the appropriate wire ends) or a unique wire color in the machine. (The diagram you are using does not use a number. However, in the electrical panel, this wire is always white. All other wires are red with a number band on their ends.)

The common grounded conductor is also shown as the direct electrical connection to one side of the output device which is being controlled on that line. (An output device is an electrical component that uses voltage to do work. It may be a relay coil, a hydraulic solenoid, a timer motor, or even a buzzer. For the purpose of definition in this book, an electrical component is the broader term which includes all switches, buttons, and whatever else is found in the circuit. The output device is specifically the electrical component which is being controlled on the right side of the ladder diagram. The symbol representation for an output device would be either a series or a shunt coil.)

The left side of the ladder is also represented by vertical lines, although these lines are not necessarily common to each other. (However, significant sections of the diagram usually are common, as you can see with wire 20 from line 47 to line 72. Refer to Appendix A.) The lines on the left-hand side will be connected to a terminal on a switch or other controlled current source.

Ladder diagram contact positions

I should stop here and make an important observation concerning the reading of the ladder diagram while doing troubleshooting. Remember, the ladder diagram is drawn as though the control voltage is *off*. In other words, the circuit is dead. So what happens when you are troubleshooting a live circuit? If activated (either electrically or mechanically), the contacts will, in fact, be in the reverse position. Let's use lines 4 and 5 in Figure 3.1 as an example. When the motor is started, push button PBM will be pressed, which will close PBM between wires B and A. PBS must also be closed between wires B and C. (Since it is a normally closed push button, that part of the circuit will be complete unless the button is pressed, or unless there is a malfunction in PBS.) LS10 must also be closed before the motor will start. This means that the rear door on the machine must be closed. Now the motor will start when the motor controller CM is energized. However, if you remove your finger from PBM, you will open the circuit and the motor will stop. So a latching circuit is provided on line 5. When CM is energized, it closes contact cm between wires B and A. This keeps the motor running until it is stopped when PBS is pressed.

If you are checking this circuit because the motor will not start—or will not continue running—you will be testing a circuit that ideally should have LS10 closed (not open as shown in the diagram). PBS should be closed (as it is in the diagram), and PBM should be closed (when starting) and cm closed (when running), although both are shown as being open in the diagram. When troubleshooting, a great deal of confusion will result if you do not keep in mind that, when energized, the contacts will be in the opposite position. Further, you will need to be able to visualize whether any given contact is to be read as energized or deenergized for the condition or setting of the machine during the actual test. [Refer back to line 4 in Figure 3.1. When the motor is running (or the circuit is energized), you cannot merely read everything as being reversed from the diagram representation. Some components will be reversed, while others will not. For example, in the normal running condition, the thermal overload for the motor (th-ry) will not have tripped—it will be in the conductive state as shown in the diagram. Equally, the stop push button [PBS] will be in the relaxed position and, therefore, will be in the conductive state as shown in the diagram. On the other hand, if the circuit has been energized and the motor is running, the rear gate safety (LS10) and the motor latching circuit contact (cm) will be energized, or closed. Thus, when you are reading a diagram during actual testing, you need to be aware of each symbol's function and decide whether it should be read as shown in the diagram, or read in its energized—or activated—mode.]

Horizontal diagram lines

The significant concept of the ladder diagram is that it represents a current path to an output device. Since an output device will control an end function (either directly through a relay or counter, or indi-

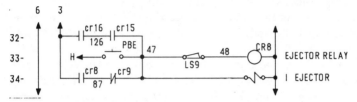

Figure 3.2   Diagram lines 32 to 35.

rectly through a pilot device such as a hydraulic control valve), a failure of that end function to activate will indicate the part of the circuit which has malfunctioned. (This is assuming, of course, that the failure was caused by the electrical control circuit.) If you know which part of the circuit has malfunctioned, you can refer to the lines in question on the ladder diagram and begin your troubleshooting procedures. You will be looking for the failure of specific switches and contacts on that line of the diagram. (You will see later that a contact not closing on the line you are checking may be caused by a malfunction on another line. Often, a relay contact is not closing on your first line, but the cause of the problem is actually on the line which is controlling the malfunctioning relay's coil.) For example, refer to the ejector section of the diagram in Figure 3.2. If the ejector does not move forward, you know that one or both of the hydraulic pilot valves (I "ejector" or J "ejector pressure" on lines 34 or 35) are not activating. Since it is a parallel circuit, you know that the problem is on lines 32, 33, 34, or 35. You would then need to check only the components on those lines—or the wires feeding those lines, which would be wires 3 and 6.

I will not stop now to explain the actual troubleshooting procedure, since you will study that in Chapter 7, Practical On-Line Troubleshooting. However, from the example you have just been given, you can see how quickly an area of the circuit can be isolated for further troubleshooting. It was isolated simply by observing the end function which did not activate—in this case, the ejector—and going quickly to that section on the ladder diagram. If you don't believe that what you have just been told is an example of "fast," then you need to spend a day watching an "expert" who doesn't need diagrams tear the innards out of both the hydraulic system and the electrical panel—and all the limit switches on the back end of the machine—only to find that there was a loose wire terminal on wire 87 on cr9 on line 34!

Understanding the Ladder Diagram

In the first chapter, you were told that good troubleshooting was based on understanding the electrical circuit as a system rather than as a series of discrete electrical components. This should become obvious to you as you study the complete ladder diagram.

The interrelated circuit diagram

The interrelatedness of the electrical system is most evident as you follow a circuit represented by one of the numbered lines. Though it is not always the case, you will most frequently find that a given line will be dependent on electrical components in other lines. In order for the relay on the line you are following to function, its circuit is dependent on a number of other relays, timers, etc., which must also operate normally. Look at Figure 3.2 again. You will see that CR8 depends on four other relays in order to function. (That is, relay contacts are shown for CR16, CR15, CR9, and CR9. Not all of these four relays are in the circuit at a given time, however. Some are only used in the automatic mode, while others are used in only the manual mode.) If you were troubleshooting this circuit because CR8 was not properly functioning, you would possibly need to troubleshoot the diagram line for any one of the other four relays. As an example, a damaged relay coil on CR16 would cause relay CR8—which you are troubleshooting—to fail in the automatic mode.

Thus, as you are learning to read ladder diagrams—and when you are actually doing the troubleshooting work in the electrical panel—you will need to be aware of the relationship of the line you are working on to other parts of the circuit on which it is dependent. Though it is not always the case, frequently relay contacts on the line you are checking are controlled by relays and switches, etc., on other lines. You will need to get used to working with multiple lines in your testing, though once you understand on-line troubleshooting, it should not present any difficulty for you.

Proper circuit grounding

Before leaving the subject of ladder diagrams, there is an area of technical information which I would like you to understand. Convention (and actual practice in the panel) always puts the electrical output device at the extreme end of the circuit; that is, next to the common grounded conductor. There is a very important safety reason for this location. Notice in Figure 3.1 that line 1 shows a ground symbol on wire G1. When the circuit is operational, SW5 is closed and the common wire is grounded to the panel. That means that the entire circuit to the left of the electrical output device is the *ungrounded* circuit. (It is the "hot" leg.) Therefore, *any short to ground in the entire circuit will blow the control transformer fuse.* (The fuse is shown on the left-hand side of the diagram between wire P1 and wire P2.)

What would happen if the output device was moved from the right side of the diagram to the left side? (For the sake of the illustration, the left side of the diagram would still be the "hot" leg.) A short to ground any place in the control circuit would *activate* the output device; the control panel chassis would complete the circuit. Can you imagine the danger that would be involved? A short circuit to ground would not blow the fuse—it would activate the circuit; a hydraulic cylinder could slam shut because of a ground fault! Equipment damage and personnel injuries would be very likely. You can see, then, why the output device is immediately adjacent to the grounded side of the circuit. Anything added to the right of the output device would cause it to function in the presence of a short to ground rather than blowing the fuse. If you ever do any add-on wiring in a panel, *always* add it on the hot side of the circuit.

Figure 3.1 also indicates that there is only one fuse on the circuit side of the control transformer. There is a fuse on the "hot" side (leg P1), but not on the grounded neutral (G1) side. Again, there is an important safety factor in this design. If a fuse was placed on the grounded side and it opened—but the fuse on the hot side remained conductive—the circuit would be inoperative, but the conductors would remain live. The circuit could not function, but it presents a hazard to anyone working on it. In practice, a fuse is never placed on the grounded side of the circuit.

Wire Diagrams

Wire diagrams will not be used for troubleshooting illustrations in this book. Nonetheless, they are a useful source of information which you will use in your electrical work.

The wire diagram's primary role is that of representing a specific—and usually limited—circuit function. In Figure 3.3 a refrigeration compressor motor circuit is shown. The purpose of this diagram is to identify the electrical functions and physical arrangement of one circuit area. To that end, the wire diagram is the best means of representation.

You will often find these diagrams in cover plates and control boxes. Frequently, there will be a wire diagram inside a magnetic motor starter cover. Because these circuits are small, it is advantageous to use physical rather than schematic diagrams. It is simpler to identify terminals and wire locations from a physical diagram. Occasionally, for equipment with simple circuits, you may find that the entire unit is represented with only a wire diagram.

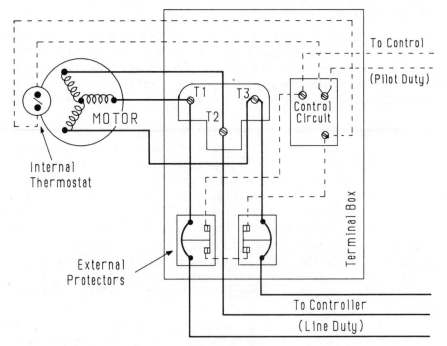

Figure 3.3   Refrigeration compressor motor wire diagram.

Very frequently, the wire diagram will include other useful information. Again, the wire diagram inside a magnetic motor starter cover will list information pertinent to that model starter such as the horsepower ratings of the starter, the overload coils to use for various current loads, and nonelectrical information such as the replacement part numbers for that particular unit. The wire diagram inside a motor cover plate may list fuse sizes or overload values relative to that particular motor. If you can decipher the fine print, there is often information on these printed diagrams which may be helpful to you in your troubleshooting work. (The solution to a motor tripping the overloads may be as simple as comparing the horsepower ratings with the overload chart in the coverplate.)

When using a wire diagram, you will read it in much the same way as you would a ladder diagram; that is, the circuit functions are represented by their appropriate symbols. However, you will need to follow conductor lines rather than a single horizontal circuit line. This will add to the potential confusion of this type of diagram. The wire diagram is a useful circuit representation. Its use, however, is generally limited to small, specific circuit functions.

Chapter Review

The ladder diagram represents the individual current paths for each of the controlled or energized electrical output devices. The current path is represented as a conductor line broken by symbol representations of each of the electrical components (relay contacts, switches, push buttons, limit switches, etc.) which are found in that particular circuit.

The value of the ladder diagram in troubleshooting is that it represents the actual circuit path you will be testing for that given machine. All of the wiring and components are represented by their unique identification numbers and symbols. The ladder diagram is a representation of the electrical function of the machine. However, it is not a representation of the actual physical layout.

The ladder diagram is always drawn in the deenergized state. (Mechanically operated devices are represented in the open or relaxed position.) When the diagram is being read in actual testing with an energized circuit, symbols must be appropriately read as being either energized or deenergized, depending on the state of that particular circuit.

The ladder diagram (and the actual circuit) always connects one leg of the electrical output devices directly to the common (and grounded) lead. This connection arrangement will blow the fuse protection (or circuit breaker) in the event of a short circuit to ground anywhere in the protected circuit. This is a mandatory safety precaution which prevents a short-to-ground from activating the output device.

The grounded (common) wire from the control transformer is never fused. Blowing a fuse on the grounded leg would deactivate the circuit, but it would create a hazard by leaving the ungrounded side of the circuit energized.

The wire diagram is generally used to represent limited circuit functions. It is a physical representation of the circuit, showing the various electrical components as they are related to each other and the conductors for that particular circuit. Wire diagrams are often found inside terminal and panel covers; they often contain specific electrical and nonelectrical information for that particular unit.

Chapter Questions

Thinking through the text

1. What is the value of the ladder diagram as a troubleshooting aid?

2. The ladder diagram represents the equipment's electrical functions, but not the physical wiring layout of the machine. Explain the difference between the electrical functions and the physical layout of electrical equipment.

3. On which side of the ladder diagram is the common conductor shown? How is it generally identified in both the drawing and the electrical panel?

4. The ladder diagram is always drawn as though the circuit is deenergized. How does this influence the way the diagram is read during testing when the control circuit is hot?

5. What is the significant concept of the ladder diagram?

6. In what way can circuits in other parts of the electrical system influence the specific circuit on which you are working? What special awareness does this necessitate?

7. Why is the output device always the last component in the circuit, with one terminal connected to the grounded (common) control wire?

8. Why is the grounded neutral leg of a control transformer never fused?

9. How does a wire diagram differ from a ladder diagram; that is, what is the difference in each diagram's form of representation?

Deepening your electrical understanding

10. The ladder diagram can be used in a number of ways to more quickly accomplish the task of electrical troubleshooting. How is it used (in conjunction with observing the machine's actual function) to determine the specific area of electrical malfunction?

11. It is mandatory that all of the electrical output devices have one of their two leads connected to the grounded (common) wire. Why? Give an example of what could happen—and why—if it is not placed in this position.

12. Can you draw a portion of Figure 3.2 as a wire diagram? Can you draw a portion of Figure 3.3 as a ladder diagram?

An On-Line Troubleshooting Overview

In this chapter you will learn how to do on-line troubleshooting by observing a working example. This troubleshooting technique will then be compared with conventional (off-line) troubleshooting to show you some of the advantages of on-line troubleshooting.

An Example of On-Line Troubleshooting

The simplest way to understand on-line troubleshooting is to see it done on a single ladder diagram line. Line 22 (Figure 4.1) has a number of switched points on it and should be relatively simple to understand. Also, for the sake of illustration, I am going to make a number of assumptions. First, I will assume that every mechanical and electrical contact is closed. (In other words, at the time of the test, CR15 will be deenergized, CR2 will be energized, S3 will be closed in the number 2 position, LS3 will be closed, CR16 will be energized, and CR8 will be deenergized. The line between wires 14 and 135 is a permanently installed jumper, so that section of the circuit should be closed.) I will also assume that wire 6, which is powering this circuit, is energized.

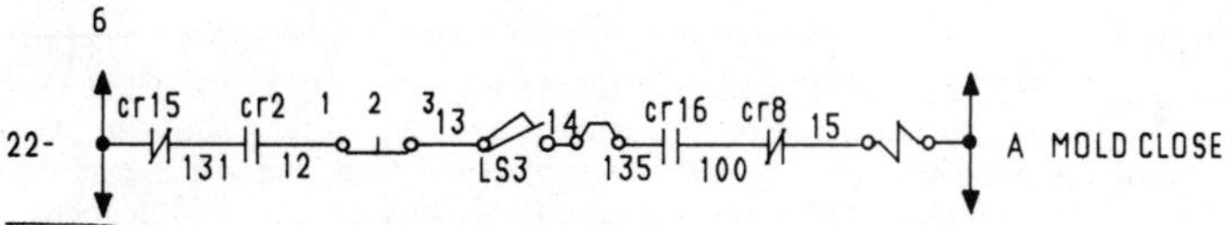

Figure 4.1 Diagram line number 22.

The machine is running, and the controls are set so that solenoid A (mold close) should energize. If the machine were functioning normally, the mold close function would sequence. However, you have an electrical problem in the machine, and the mold-close solenoid A is not functioning; the hydraulic pumps are running but the machine is stalled.

In actual practice, you would now do a preliminary check of the machine. (This will be covered in Chapter 6, Collecting Information.) For this illustration, however, I will assume that you found nothing in your visual inspection of the machine that indicates a problem. Your next step is to study the ladder diagram to determine the non-functioning area. Since the mold is not closing when it should, you can isolate solenoid A on line 22 as the problem area. (Make a careful distinction at this point between an electrical component which is not functioning and a component which is faulty. The mold is not closing because solenoid A is not functioning. This is not saying, however, that the solenoid itself is at fault. The fault may be anything in the mechanical or electrical system which prevents the control voltage from reaching the solenoid.)

The troubleshooting process

You are going to troubleshoot line 22 (Figure 4.1). However, your procedure will be different from that of most of your fellow electricians. (They would probably stop the machine and check the wiring for open circuits.) For your on-line troubleshooting, you will proceed as follows (see Figure 4.2):

Step 1.   You will set up the machine under power so that the mold should close; the motor is running, the control circuit is on, and the control selectors are set so that solenoid A should be energized.

Step 2.   You will start your actual diagnostic work by testing the circuit for continuity. (Yes, continuity! I did not forget that the lines are hot. However, you will be using a Hioki Pencil Hi Tester digital multimeter—or an equivalent meter from another supplier—which can test resistance and continuity with up to 250 V on the line. Or, you may be using a Greenlee BEHA Unitest 575 voltage and continuity tester which is designed to read continuity on a live circuit with up to 600 V.[1] This is the key to the speed of on-line troubleshooting.

---

[1] In Chapter 1, Getting Started with Electrical Troubleshooting, you studied some important safety procedures. Be certain that you understand all necessary precautions before working in a live panel. Do not attempt any testing until you know that you are adequately protected from all controlled (higher) voltages, and that you will be using your test equipment on no more than 120 V control circuits for any on-line troubleshooting tests.

Figure 4.2 Testing a live circuit in an electrical panel. As illustrated here, complete circuits in other parts of the machine may be tested from readily accessible terminal blocks. (*A. W. Sperry Instruments, Inc.*)

On-line troubleshooting can also be done with other test equipment. I will explain those alternatives later in the book.)

Before going further, I need to give you a definition of continuity. A circuit with continuity provides a continuous path along which an electric current can pass. Stated another way, a conductor or a circuit has continuity when a current can be passed through that conductor (or circuit) encountering no significantly greater resistance than is in the wiring and the components of the circuit itself. A conductor has continuity. A nonconductor (for whatever reason) does not have continuity. Obviously, then, when you are testing a control circuit, it must have continuity before it can function; that is, it must carry current to the intended electrical output device.

You should also be aware that a standard ohmmeter cannot be used for continuity testing on a live circuit. Unless your meter was specifically designed for live circuit testing on the ohm or continuity settings, do not attempt to read resistance or check for a completed circuit unless you know the circuit you are testing is entirely disconnected.

Step 3.   Until you verify individual components on the machine itself, almost all of your testing will be done from inside the electrical panel. These techniques will be explained in later parts of the book. (Not only will you learn how to test various components which are outside of the electrical panel, but in Chapter 9, Specialized Tests and Equipment, you will discover ways to actually verify mechanical functions—such as a solenoid valve's operation—from inside the panel.)

Remember that the entire line 22 needs to act as a single conductor in order for solenoid A to function. This means that from any point on the left-side terminal of the solenoid (wire 15) to any point along the entire circuit of line 22, you should be able to read continuity with your meter. However, since the solenoid is not energized, you will expect to find some point at which there is an open circuit. That, in fact, is the purpose of your test; to find the point along line 22 at which continuity is broken.

Actual testing

You are now ready to start the actual testing from inside the panel. (Most of the testing will be done from the numbered terminal blocks, though occasionally you will test from numbered wires on relays, timers, or other circuit components.) Your testing sequence will be as follows:

Test 1.   Your first, and only voltage test, is from wire 6 to the common grounded conductor on the right-hand side of solenoid A.

Purpose.   To verify the presence of a control voltage.

Test results.   Your meter indicates 120 V. Continue with the next test sequence.

Test 2.   Change your meter setting to continuity. Test solenoid A for an open circuit by touching the leads to the common grounded conductor and wire 15. (For the purpose of this illustration, the ladder diagram has been altered. The complete diagram shows relay CR9 as common to solenoid A with a common grounded conductor 15. If you were to test for continuity between wire 15 and the common wire, you would be testing a parallel circuit for both solenoid A and CR9. This parallel circuit would give you a reading even if solenoid A was removed from the circuit. In actual testing, there are simple procedures which will allow you to verify each of them separately. For now, however, use the diagram as though wire 15 is not common to any other parallel circuit.)

Purpose.   To verify a complete circuit for solenoid A (mold close).

Test results.   Beep = continuity. (You now know that the solenoid and its circuits are operational. Your meter indicates continuity with a beep tone.)

Test 3.   Arbitrarily select a midpoint connection for line 22. Wire 14 is on the terminal block and is convenient to use, so test for continuity from the previous test point (wire 15) and the terminal block wire 14.

Purpose.   To test the jumper connection (wire 14 to wire 135), relay contact cr16, relay contact cr8, and all terminal connections between the two points.

Test results.   Beep = continuity. (You now know that all contacts and terminals are operational between wires 14 and 15.)

Test 4.   Now test the other half of the circuit for continuity by testing from terminal block wire 14 to wire 6.

Purpose.   To test LS3, selector switch S3, relay contacts cr2 and cr15, and all terminal connections between the two points.

Test result.   No beep = open circuit. (You now know that an electrical component or connection between wire 14 and wire 6 is faulty or open.)

Test 5.   Test between wire 14 and wire 13 on the electrical panel terminal block.

Purpose.   To verify LS3 and its connections.

Test result.   Beep = continuity. (You now know that limit switch LS3 and its connections form a completed circuit.)

Test 6.   Test between wire 13 and wire 12 on the electrical panel terminal block.

Purpose.   To verify selector switch S3 and its connections.

Test result.   No beep = open circuit. (You now know that either the switch or the wiring is defective between these two points. You will need to go to the control panel to make the verification, since this part of the circuit is on the machine itself. However, before you do, make one last test from the electrical panel to make certain that there is only one area at fault.)

Test 7.   Test between wire 12 and wire 6 on the electrical panel terminal block.

Purpose.   To verify relay contacts cr15 and cr2.

Test result.   Beep = continuity. (Both relay contacts are operational. You now know that the fault is in selector switch S3 or its connections.)

Test 8.   Open the operator's control panel and locate the back of selector switch S3. Locate wire 12 and wire 13.

Purpose.   To verify that either the switch S3—or its connections— are faulty.

Test result.   Touch the test leads to the switch terminals (not the wire ends). The absence of a beep would verify a faulty switch. Continuity would indicate a poor wire connection.

You have now found the cause of the malfunction on line 22. It is either a faulty switch (S3) or a poor connection on one of the switch terminals. If you suspect a loose terminal screw, you would turn off the power and tighten the connections with a screwdriver. Remember, to this point you have been working on a hot circuit! You could verify the lack of continuity across the S3 terminals by jumping across wires 12 and 13 with a short piece of insulated wire. With the machine running and in an operation mode, you would expect to see the mold close. Your tests will now verify that either the terminal contacts to S3 or the switch itself is faulty. The rest of the job will follow standard repair procedures. Turn the power off before doing any repair work.

At this point, I need to remind you of a very necessary safety precaution. During on-line troubleshooting, the machine is in an operation mode while you are doing the testing. There are two safety areas that must concern you:

1. You are working on live circuits. Don't get sloppy! (In some cases, that may involve only a 24-V control circuit. Personal risk is greatly reduced at the lower voltages. Nonetheless, carelessness still poses the very real threat of damage to the electrical equipment by short circuiting the control circuits with the test probes.

2. Be certain at all times that the machine is properly cleared so that it could continue its cycle with neither personnel injury nor damage

to the machine. This is necessary because, in the process of testing, you may jiggle a loose contact and cause the machine to cycle. If you have taken the proper safety precautions, that in itself is a useful part of the testing; you have found the loose connection that was causing the problem. But if you have been careless, that cycle could cause personnel or equipment damage.

A review of on-line troubleshooting

Let's do a quick review of the on-line troubleshooting procedure you just finished.

First, you purposely put the machine in the running mode (most likely in an actual automatic cycle setting) and let it reach a point at which it would not continue its normal operating sequence. At the point at which the machine stalls, you can much more easily determine the area of fault. Checking a stalled machine will usually result in your being able to quickly isolate an output device (such as the mold closing solenoid in the example) which is not functioning. (The device is not functioning, though the device itself may be fully operational.)

By leaving the machine stalled while it is still in the running mode, you can follow the ladder diagram and check the circuit for open conditions. This is conveniently done by subdividing the circuit and checking for continuity. At some point, you will find a section of the circuit which is open; you can then test specific components on that circuit until you isolate an individual faulty component or connection.

For the sake of clarity, I need to restate an important part of the testing procedure. In some cases, you will actually be doing your testing while the machine is in normal operation. In this case, it is obvious that all control settings, safety gates, and any other electrical equipment involved in the circuits you will be testing are in their normal positions. Thus, any testing will, in fact, be on a fully operational circuit. (This will often be the case when you are checking a function which is not critical to the machine's main operation—such as an air blast ejection system.) However, when you are operating a machine until it stalls (which means it has reached a point in its automatic cycle at which it will not continue because some mechanical or electrical function has not sequenced) you will want to leave it in exactly that operating mode while you do your testing. That means nothing is changed on the machine or the operator's panel from the time the machine stalled until you are through with that portion of the online troubleshooting. For instance, if you open a safety gate, turn a selector switch to the manual position, etc., you will change the circuit in the panel, and you will no longer be doing on-line trouble-shooting.

It is important that both you and the operators understand the procedure. If you are anticipating testing a piece of equipment, you will need to carefully explain to the operators that when the machine ceases to function normally, they are to call you without touching any control or part of the machine. Of course, you understand that this does not bypass necessary safety precautions. However, particularly when you are testing intermittent failures (which you may not be able to reproduce at will), it is mandatory that you begin testing the electrical circuit in precisely the mode it failed.

Finally, you can do the majority of the testing from the electrical panel rather than moving from switch to switch on the machine. Testing individual switches or components is often done with considerable effort in exposing the switches and their wiring terminals. Only as a last step do you need to open operator control panels or limit switch mounting boards to verify your testing. (Or possibly to select between a small number of switches which do not have individual wiring to the electrical panel.)

What did you gain by the procedure you just used? Speed! The entire procedure described in the example should have taken no more than 10 or 15 minutes for the actual testing even if there was no prior knowledge of a malfunctioning selector switch.

Comparing Other Troubleshooting Methods

By this time you should have a basic understanding of how you will be testing with on-line troubleshooting. You will be testing for continuity (open circuits) in a circuit that is live. The machinery may even be in production. It is a live circuit because you want to test the circuit under its actual running conditions. That is the simplest and fastest way to find what is not operating normally.

Conventional troubleshooting methods

Conventional troubleshooting, however, is generally done off-line. In other words, the control circuit is deenergized. (Every troubleshooter has a personal technique, but some form of off-line diagnosis is the most frequently used.) The primary reason for deenergized control systems is the need to accommodate older-style volt-ohmmeters. Until recently, it was not possible to use standard test meters for a continuity check on live circuits. A significant part of the check can in fact be done with a voltmeter. Nonetheless, it would mean switching back and forth between volt and ohm functions on the meter, while turning the electrical control circuit power on and off. Because of the potential of error and the resulting damage to equipment—and electricians!—most test procedures have been standardized, to a large extent, as off-line.

Because the control circuit is off in conventional testing, "jumping" becomes a standard practice. If you want to make a continuity test with the control circuit dead in a circuit which has a relay electrically holding a contact closed, you must either mentally calculate the effect of that open contact or you must physically complete the circuit with an auxiliary—or jumper—wire.

Advantages of on-line troubleshooting

In electrical troubleshooting, the effectiveness of a testing procedure has as much to do with the person doing the work as it does with the procedure itself. Other techniques besides what I am suggesting here are effectively used every day by qualified electricians in industry. Nonetheless, with the solid-state tools which are available today, there are some distinct advantages in doing continuity testing while the equipment is on-line. The profitability advantage is almost always found in faster diagnosis and less downtime. With speed as the end result (and with no sacrifice in safety when the procedure is properly done), let's compare on-line troubleshooting with more conventional methods. The following are some of the advantages that come with the use of on-line troubleshooting:

Downtime is reduced or eliminated.   Many times a troublesome electrical function is not going to shut equipment down, but it nonetheless needs to be corrected. The easiest way to do on-line troubleshooting is from inside the electrical panel while the machinery is running. (As always, poor safety procedures are not allowable. I am assuming that the electrical panel is properly constructed with no more than 120 V as the control voltage and that there are appropriate clearances from the higher voltages being controlled.) The advantage is then very obvious because this troubleshooting technique will often allow diagnosis without taking machinery off-line until the actual replacement of a faulty electrical component is made.

Electrical components can be tested under load.   Shutting equipment down electrically for testing will always introduce some degree of variation in the circuit as compared with its operation under load. Loose terminals, pitted contacts, or weak contact springs may all operate differently with the power off. A loose terminal may easily carry the current from an ohmmeter, though it would not carry the actual control current. This is particularly true in the case of relay contacts.

With the circuit live, the contacts will be properly sequenced and under normal load. It is only then that the relay contacts themselves can be properly included in the test. (We have all done it—testing through a dead circuit from the relay contact terminals to the rest of the circuit and finding nothing wrong. Later we find out through much trial and error that the cause of the problem is a single set of relay contacts that we had not tested because the continuity test was done from the relay terminal.) Even if the contacts themselves are not faulty, it is much simpler to test a circuit with the contacts in their proper operating positions than to work through the wiring diagram and mentally figuring their sequence.

Intermittent problems can be found more quickly.   Probably the hardest troubleshooting task for any electrician is an intermittent fault. It is usually the result of a loose connection or a failing relay or switching contact. Frequently, when doing off-line troubleshooting, the very procedure of turning off the power (or at least removing the operating load from the circuit) will offer enough variation to temporarily allow the component to carry enough current to indicate a positive reading with an ohmmeter. The result can be either a great deal of lost time trying to find the failing component, or the expensive and unnecessary replacement of a number of components in the circuit.

With on-line troubleshooting, you set the conditions to do the testing on a live circuit that is in the actual process of failing. By allowing the machine to run until it stalls (that is, until it will not continue to sequence), you are testing all of the electrical components and circuits under actual operating conditions. If it is an intermittent failure (assuming that safety is not compromised), you can put the machine back into operation and wait until it fails. (Waiting by a running machine so that it will fail can be a time-consuming experience. It may be anywhere from a few minutes of operation to months. You are going to waste a lot of time trying to find an electrical fault that doesn't presently exist.) When the fault does occur, without changing any of the settings, you can proceed with the testing knowing that there is, in fact, a circuit failure that will be evident.

Intermittent problems are often related to high resistance in relay or switch contacts. If you are using one of the recommended test meters capable of doing on-line troubleshooting, you may find a further diagnostic aid in its tone response. Some meters will vary their tone in the continuity setting when resistances are higher than 100 or 200 Ω. The resistance value of closed relay contacts should be much lower. A faltering tone variation in the continuity setting may indicate potential high resistance which is a clue to a failing contact. I cannot give you a rule to follow at this point, as each meter will respond differently. Get used to your own meter, however, and you may find that the tone will give you additional information.

Electrical safety may be enhanced.   On the surface, it would appear that working on a live electrical circuit increases accident potential. That is certainly true when hazardous and sloppy procedures are used. However, there are areas in which more traditional troubleshooting can introduce its own hazard potentials. The most obvious is when jumper leads are used to complete tests. Even if the circuit is dead, it requires adding wires (with clips!) into a panel that was not designed for them. If the circuit is energized for temporary testing, there is a very real hazard of shock or damage resulting from faulty connections. Jumping across contacts with a live circuit not only runs the risk of short circuits but also introduces the potential of closing circuits that jeopardize safety (of either personnel or the machine) because they are out of sequence. (Jumping, in effect, can remove electrical interlocks. If the machine is being tested using on-line troubleshooting techniques while it is in operation, that is not possible.) With on-line troubleshooting, you are not altering or adding wiring to the manufacturer's circuit. Further, electrical safety functions will not be bypassed, nor can the machine be dangerously sequenced.

Thus, on-line troubleshooting has some decided advantages which evidence themselves in faster electrical diagnosis. At the same time, not only does it maintain electrical safety practices when properly done, but on-line troubleshooting may enhance safety by preserving the manufacturer's wiring and electrical sequences even during testing.

Chapter Review

On-line troubleshooting is done with the machine or electrical equipment in the running mode. The equipment is either cycled in its normal operation mode, or it is operated until it stalls (that is, until it will not continue to the next operational sequence). Troubleshooting is then done on the live circuit in an attempt to isolate a single malfunction in the control circuit.

On-line troubleshooting is ideally done as a continuity test on the live circuit. Test equipment is used which can tolerate line voltage during a continuity or resistance test. Troubleshooting is carried out by first testing large sections of the faulty circuit for continuity. When there is continuity, the procedure is carried out on adjacent sections of the circuit. When lack of continuity is indicated, circuit sections are subdivided until the subcircuit area is found where there is a break in continuity.

Safety is a major concern of any troubleshooting procedure. In the case of on-line troubleshooting, in addition to the care taken while working on live circuits, there is the need for special precaution to avoid personnel or machine damage caused by inadvertent machine cycling during testing.

On-line troubleshooting offers some definite advantages over conventional troubleshooting. Downtime can be greatly reduced or, in some cases, eliminated entirely. Electrical components can be more accurately tested under actual load. Intermittent problems can be found more easily under live circuit operating conditions. Finally, electrical troubleshooting safety may actually be enhanced because the need for electrically jumping circuits is eliminated.

Chapter Questions

Thinking through the text

1. How are the machine controls set for on-line troubleshooting?

2. Define *continuity*.

3. Two safety precautions are mentioned which must be uppermost in your mind when you are conducting on-line troubleshooting tests. What are they? What are the possible consequences of their violation?

4. On-line troubleshooting is often done when the equipment is "stalled." Describe a stalled machine according to the definition of the text. In what position are the controls when the equipment is stalled?

5. What is "jumping"? How is it used? How can it increase the potential of danger?

Deepening your electrical understanding

6. Both on-line troubleshooting and conventional troubleshooting test the circuit for breaks in what should be a single conductor if the circuit were in normal operation. In standard testing procedures, you would use a voltmeter to read zero volts when there is no "open" in the conductor. Can you diagrammatically show how a zero voltmeter reading can be obtained: (a) when the

live circuit you are testing is complete (this will represent an accurate test reading) and (*b*) when the live circuit you are testing is "open" (this will represent a false test reading)?

7.   How will a continuity (rather than voltmeter) test result in greater reliability? Can you demonstrate this by showing what a continuity reading would indicate on part (*b*) of question 6?

8.   Why is a continuity test on a stalled machine such an advantage in locating intermittent circuit problems? What is the purpose in allowing the machine to stall?

5

On-Line
Troubleshooting Tools

*In this chapter you will be introduced to some of
the equipment currently available for electrical
troubleshooting. This will include both contact
testers (instruments which are used in contact with
live circuits) and noncontact testers (instruments
which measure the conductor's electrical field). The
advantages and uses of various instruments will be
discussed.*

A New Generation of Test Equipment

Something dramatic has happened in the field of test equipment. With
the advent of microelectronics, a generation of hand-held meters is
now available with testing capabilities unheard of relatively few
years ago. As an example, one supplier's hand-held clamp-on ammeter
(Hioki's digital clamp-on Hi Tester 3261 shown in Figure 5.1) can read
from 0.01[1] to 1,000 A, from 1 to 1,000 V, from 1 to 10 KΩ, and with a
thermocouple attachment it can read temperature. But that is not all.
In either the volt or amp range it can be set to read the actual line
value, the average value for a set time, or the peak value. As if that
were not enough, it can also be used to read frequency from 10 to 300
Hz. (Other companies produce comparable equipment.)

Helping you improve your speed and accuracy when you troubleshoot is a major objective of this book. Your troubleshooting effectiveness will not only be a function of your testing procedures, it will also
be a result of the equipment you are using. The explosion of new elec-

---

[1] 0.01 A is not a misprint. This incredible meter has a 1 to 1,000 normal range ammeter and a 0.00 multiplier range which reads the value to two decimal places. In Chapter 9 you will see how this low range can be advantageously used.

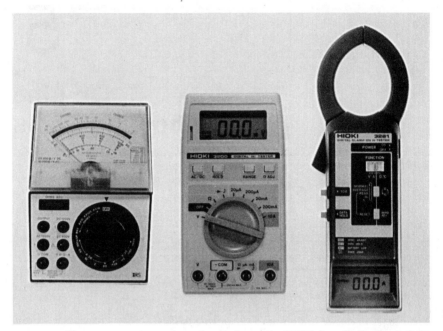

Figure 5.1   Three common test meters. A volt-ohmmeter (VOM) from Radio Shack (left), a digital voltmeter (DVM) from Hioki (center), and a clamp-on ammeter from Hioki (right). (*From Radio Shack Division of Tandy Corp., and Hioki-RCC, Inc.*)

tronic diagnostic equipment is bringing the potential of amazing speed and accuracy to the maintenance electrician's normal working day. As this chapter—and the remainder of the book—is developed, you will be introduced to some of these test instruments.

Electronic test equipment makes new methods possible

In spite of the new equipment which is now available, many of the testing procedures for the plant maintenance electrician still unnecessarily rely on the methods previously required by D'Arsonval moving coil volt-ohmmeters. For instance, continuity readings are still done as though the circuit must be dead. With some of the new electronic equipment, however, continuity checks can now be made on live circuits.

Furthermore, the full capability of much of the new equipment is not being satisfactorily utilized. You will later see how a megohmmeter can be used to verify a motor while it is still in the circuit (and probably even hidden in the machinery 20 feet away!). The megohmmeter can do much more than bench-test a motor's insulation or give routine data for motor maintenance records. It can become a rather spectacular troubleshooting tool with the potential of significant time savings; a suspect motor can be quickly checked from the magnetic starter's terminals.

There is a use for this new generation of equipment, however, that goes far beyond novelty. These test instruments can bring a dramatic decrease in the time spent locating electrical problems during troubleshooting. That, of course, translates into greater equipment productivity in the plant. The electrician who can significantly reduce machine downtime in today's manufacturing economy has made great personal strides toward professional advancement as well as increasing the employer's profitability.

The value of this new test equipment goes beyond mere speed. There is less teardown to expose machinery, less contact with circuits, and less time spent working in the electrical panel, which can all lead to greater personnel and equipment safety. The use of this new generation of test equipment can often reduce the hazards associated with electrical maintenance work.

Choosing test instruments

You will see numerous references to specific brand names and model numbers of electrical test instruments in this book, particularly in this chapter and Chapter 9, Specialized Tests and Equipment. I have done this of necessity; some of the troubleshooting I am demonstrating requires meter capabilities found in these specific test instruments. I have mentioned these meters because it serves the purpose of identifying a specific meter function for a given testing procedure.

However, my purpose in listing brand names and models is not to limit the test equipment which you might use to those mentioned in this book. Rather, through this kind of identification, you will be able to locate other test instruments which will accomplish the same testing functions. The information given in these chapters should help you in your evaluation of any make of test instrument.

Nonetheless, I have used each of the test instruments I have named and can recommend them as excellent meters for the job for which they are described.

Contact and Noncontact Measurements

Electrical measurement is essentially achieved in one of two ways. Probably the most common measurement method is contact testing. In contact testing, leads or probes of the meter make electrical contact with the conductors of the circuit under test. The circuit may be energized or deenergized, the distinction being that the circuit of the meter is electrically common to the conductors of the circuit. The second method is noncontact testing. In noncontact testing, the internal circuit of the meter is isolated from the conductor(s) of the circuit under test. In this case, the meter is sensitive to an electromagnetic field surrounding the conductor. (The current may be induced in the meter by transformer action as is done with a clamp-on ammeter, or the meter may be sensitive to capacitance changes or other properties of an electromagnetic field.)

Contact testing

Volt-ohmmeters (VOMs) (which are moving-coil analog meters with needle and scale indicators) or digital voltmeters (DVMs) (which are electronic meters with solid-state circuits and a digital readout display), are probably the most recognizable instruments used for contact testing. (Refer to Figure 5.1.) All standard tests using these instruments are done by touching their leads to the actual electrical circuit. The electrical circuit (whether a hot lead or a chassis ground) is thus common to the internal circuit of the VOM or DVM. This is true of any measurement done with a VOM or DVM, whether voltage, resistance, or—as provided on some instruments—milliamperage. (Some multimeters have temperature or clamp-on ammeter attachments. These fall outside of the normal use of a VOM or DVM, though they still rely on the meter's voltage ranges and are thus technically contact testing insofar as the meter itself is concerned. In these cases, the attachment produces a voltage which is common to the circuit of the multimeter.) Many other tests are also made through direct contact with the circuit being tested. Capacitor testers, continuity testers, and phase rotation indicators are examples of test equipment which require direct contact with the circuit during the test.

Noncontact testing

The clamp-on ammeter, on the other hand, is probably the best known example of a noncontact test instrument. (A clamp-on ammeter is shown in Figure 5.1.) In order to take a reading, the ammeter's laminated jaw is clamped around an alternating current conductor; no physical connection with the live circuit is required. A current is induced in an internal winding in the ammeter itself, though the ammeter's circuit is completely isolated from the circuit being tested. (The ammeter is really a secondary transformer connected to the instrument's moving coil or digital readout which is calibrated to show ampere values. The finely wound coil at the bottom of the jaw is the transformer secondary, and the conductor clamped in the jaw is the transformer primary.) Many other types of testers have been built which use some form of induced or capacitive interaction with an insulated conductor so that a value in the conductor can be read without electrical contact with the circuit in the conductor. Safety and the ease of use are the primary considerations behind the development of noncontact test equipment.

Although this section has introduced the two types of instruments as though all meters are exclusively contact or noncontact, there are, in fact, a number of combination meters on the market. Probably the most frequently seen is the clamp-on ammeter (which is a noncontact meter) with a built-in voltmeter or even a volt-ohmmeter (which requires leads and therefore would be a contact meter). There are other interesting combination meters such as TIF Instrument's Tic Tracer 300 (Figure 5.2). The primary instrument is a noncontact proximity

Figure 5.2 Two combination meters from TIF; a capacitor/continuity tester TIF660 (*left*) and a proximity voltage/continuity tester TIF300CC (*right*). (*TIF Instruments, Inc.*)

meter which detects the presence of an AC voltage. Built into the meter, however, are leads (and circuitry) which are used for contact continuity testing.

Moving-Coil Meters

Before moving on to digital and solid-state equipment, let's stop for a brief look at the workhorse of electrical testing equipment. The multimeter you are undoubtedly most familiar with has a needle which swings in an arc across a scale. Figure 5.3 shows the internal construction of a D'Arsonval (or analog) moving-coil meter. (This type of meter is classified as a permanent-magnet moving-coil meter.)

Moving-coil meter construction

It may help you to understand the function of the moving-coil meter by comparing it to a permanent-magnet DC motor. Like a DC motor, the D'Arsonval meter movement has a fine wire-wound armature that is free to rotate. (Unlike a motor, however, the armature has a fixed rotation limit of about 90°.) In the most common meter arrangement, the electrical current is commutated to the armature through two spiral springs (rather than through brushes as in a DC motor). When a DC current of the correct polarity is applied to the armature, the armature will rotate clockwise. However, since the armature is opposed by the spiral wound springs, the amount of rotation is dependent on the magnetic field strength of the armature. The field strength is a function of the applied current; the higher the current, the greater the deflection of the needle.[2]

---

[2] An explanation is needed in order to avoid confusion when talking about the moving-coil meter's response. A D'Arsonval moving-coil meter is sensitive to current, not voltage. However, the value imposed on the moving coil in almost all VOMs is always a voltage value. A short history note is in order. One of the most important discoveries in the history of electricity was that of electromagnetism by Hans Christian Oersted in 1819. In 1820 he published a short paper describing the magnetic field surrounding a conductor; it was the application of this discovery which allowed the development of induction and magnetic equipment in the field of electricity. Oersted accurately described the force between the conductor and the magnet as being a function of current and not voltage. How, then, does the moving-coil meter vary with a change in voltage? The answer is an application of Ohm's law, which tells us that the current in an electrical circuit is directly proportional to the voltage in the circuit (and inversely proportional to the resistance in the circuit). Therefore, if the voltage value increases, the current value will also increase. Thus, the meter can respond to voltage because an increase in voltage will increase the current, which in turn increases the magnetic flux causing the needle movement. For the sake of accuracy, this chapter generally refers to the moving coil as responding to current even though the value being measured is, in most cases, voltage.

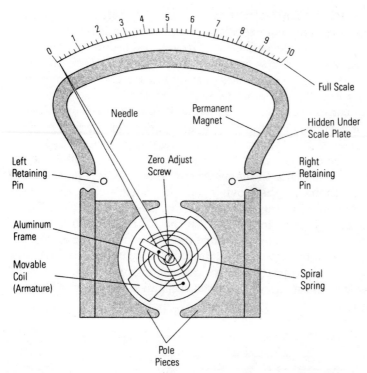

Figure 5.3   The internal construction of a typical D'Arsonval moving-coil meter movement. (*From Radio Shack Division of Tandy Corp. Used by permission.*)

A high-quality VOM uses a very sensitive moving coil. Calibrated springs and a balanced coil and needle result in a linear deflection of the needle across the scale as the current in the coil is increased linearly (which means that the deflection of the needle is in exact ratio to the amount of applied current). An aluminum frame is used which provides a dampening action on the needle movement. (The frame, in effect, is a single-turn conductor. As the shorted conductor moves in the magnetic field, a voltage is induced in the aluminum frame. The induced voltage requires work energy, which in turn dampens the movement of the needle, keeping it from overshooting and oscillating.)

A very small DC current is required for full-scale deflection of the moving-coil meter (usually in the range of 50 or 100 mA). To appreciate the sensitivity of the coil, look at the lowest DC voltage range on your meter. Since even the lowest DC range in most meters has series resistance in the meter's circuit, you know that the actual maximum allowable voltage to the coil is less than that of the scale value. In most cases, full-scale deflection in the lowest range would require no greater than 0.6 V. (The sensitivity of a given meter is often a measure of its quality. The more sensitive the meter, the less current that is required for full-scale deflection. Greater sensitivity is achieved with more turns of finer wire on the armature winding. Greater meter sensitivity means that the meter is putting less load on the circuit it is testing, which results in a more accurate reading.)

All meter operations, whether in the measurement of AC or DC volts, resistance, or current, are a function of an applied voltage to the armature of the moving coil. (The maximum voltage may be less than 0.5 V DC.) It should be obvious, then, that the function of the meter selector switch is to add resistance to the meter circuit so that it can reduce the voltage to safe limits for the moving coil. (As noted earlier in the footnote, this reduction of voltage through series resistance has the effect of reducing the coil current.) In addition, on the AC ranges, a bridge rectifier is also put into the circuit to change the AC to DC. In the case of the resistance ranges, a battery circuit is included which provides the power for the moving coil. Ammeter ranges are comprised of shunt resistors which allow the voltage drop across the resistance elements to be measured. Figure 5.4 shows a typical VOM circuit schematic.

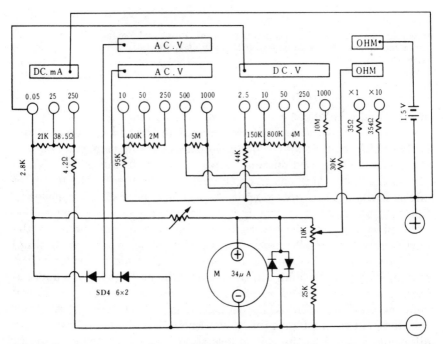

Figure 5.4 A typical moving-coil volt-ohmmeter circuit schematic. (*Courtesy of A. W. Sperry, Inc.*)

Reading the moving-coil meter

Meter accuracy is dependent upon two factors, one of which you can control on the meter itself. The first factor that affects the VOM's accuracy is the quality of the design and construction. You will get what you pay for, but beyond that, you cannot increase an existing meter's internal accuracy. However, in using a meter, you can control its accuracy by properly selecting the range on which you take a reading. For a given VOM, the accuracy will be stated as a percentage of the full-scale reading. For example, if you have a meter rated at 1 percent accuracy, you would get the following results for a 2-V reading on the 10-V scale, the 5-V scale, and the 2.5-V scale. If you were reading 2 V on a 10-V scale, the accuracy would be +0.1 V (5 percent). If you took the same 2-V reading on the 5-V scale, the accuracy would be +0.05 V (2.5 percent). Finally, if you took the 2-V reading on the 2.5-V scale, the accuracy would be +0.025 V (1.25 percent). Thus, the most accurate readings will be those which are the closest to the full-scale value of the meter. Readings at the lowest end of the scale are the least accurate. This is true of any reading, whether it is volts, ohms, or amps.

[There is a type of moving-coil meter which can read very high resistance values with great accuracy. The typical VOM meter uses a series meter, which means that the resistance being measured is in series with the coil. This meter will always read a high resistance value at the left of the scale and a low value at the right of the scale. However, for accurate readings of high resistance values, a shunt ohmmeter is often used. In this meter, the resistance being measured is in parallel with the coil. The result of this circuit change is that the greatest needle deflection (where the meter is the most accurate) is achieved with high-resistance measurements. The shunt meter will almost always reverse the scale from a standard series meter scale. That is, the shunt meter will show zero resistance on the left of the scale and infinity (∞) on the right of the scale.]

It would be worthwhile to review the difference between the DC and AC voltage reading on a VOM or DVM. The DC voltage scale represents the potential difference between the two measurement points. If a 1.5-V battery is being measured, the voltage difference between the two terminals is shown as the DC voltage on the meter scale. This is not the case with AC voltage. The standard AC voltage available for consumer and most industrial usage in the United States and Canada is a 60-cycle sine wave. (Most European, African, and Asian countries use a 50-cycle sine wave.) However, the sine wave passes through two zero points on each cycle. (Sixty-cycle current has 120 zero points and 120 full-voltage peaks each second.) Therefore, a voltage reading of 120 V AC is an effective voltage of 120 V, not a peak of 120 V. AC effective voltage is defined as the value of alternating current or voltage which will produce the same heating effect as would be produced by an equal value of direct current or voltage. For a sine wave, the effective voltage is equal to 0.707 times the peak value. (This is the RMS, or root-mean-square, value.) Or, stated in peak voltage values, a 60-cycle sine wave must reach a peak voltage of approximately 170 V to equal the heating effect of a 120-V DC voltage. (European voltage standards vary, although 220 V is becoming more common. Using the same 0.707 value for 220 V and a 50-cycle sine wave gives a peak value of approximately 312 V.) Since AC voltage is defined as an RMS value (that is, the effective voltage value), meters are scaled to read this equivalent value. The actual voltage value is alternating between zero and 170 V; for convenience, however, your meter will represent that value as a constant 120 AC voltage. (Or, if you are reading a 220-V reading, the values are alternating between zero and approximately 312 V.)

Using a moving-coil meter

You should also be aware of several precautions in handling and using a VOM. When you are measuring unknown values of voltage or current, always start at the highest ranges. (In other words, do a first measurement of an unknown AC voltage with the function selector switch set on 600 V AC. Subsequently, you can set the function selector on the appropriate range after first reading the voltage on the 600-V scale.) This protects the meter from excessive voltages. Do not change the function selector switch while the meter is under load. (Induction in the circuit you are measuring may create a high-voltage spike when the meter function selector switch is moved, particularly in the resistance ranges.) When measuring DC voltages, start at a high value and momentarily touch the probes to the circuit. Watch the direction of the needle's deflection. If it is in the reverse direction, change the polarity of the probes before continuing the testing. (Setting the meter on the high range protects the coil from damage by subjecting it to full voltage in a reverse-polarity mode.) Probably the most important operating rule for all VOMs (and most DVMs) is to use the resistance settings on dead circuits only. (In this book there are frequent references to continuity checks on live circuits. This must not be done with a moving-coil VOM. Reading a voltage with the meter on a resistance setting will either blow the overload protection—usually a replaceable fuse—or destroy the meter if it is not protected.) When you have finished using a VOM, turn the function selector switch to the off position or the highest voltage setting. Never leave a VOM in the resistance settings, both because there is danger to the meter if the probes accidently come in contact with a live circuit, and because it will drain the batteries while in storage.

In spite of the emphasis in this book on newer electronic test equipment, the VOM is still a valuable instrument. When properly used, it is capable of a wide range of troubleshooting procedures and is a valuable tool for the maintenance electrician.

Troubleshooting with a VOM or DVM

Most industrial troubleshooting work done with either a VOM or a DVM will be voltage (both AC and DC, though AC is probably the most frequently tested) or low-resistance scale tests (which includes continuity). (Most use of the resistance function of the ohmmeter in industrial electrical work will be on the X1 scale. Most resistance testing is done to determine whether a circuit is either open or has continuity. In these cases, the reading will either be infinity for an open circuit or a reading of a very few ohms for a completed circuit.)

Internal VOM or DVM ammeter ranges (usually in milliamperes) are primarily used in electronic rather than electrical work. Industrial electrical tests usually require ammeter ranges into the tens and hundreds of amps. (For example, a 10-hp, three-phase motor running at full load on 240-V service would draw approximately 18 A. Power factor and efficiency losses would add additional current draw. The starting current would be approximately six times the full-load running current or 108 A.) Needless to say, the internal ampere ranges of VOMs and DVMs cannot be used on these high values.

Most DVMs perform the same testing functions as their VOM counterparts, though with a lower percentage of internal error (which was discussed earlier) and greater reading accuracy. (The reading accuracy is greater because your eye is incapable of distinguishing between small interval variations of a needle on a scale. In contrast, the DVM will read the number to two, three, or more significant digits). Unless specified otherwise, the same meter precautions for measuring dead circuits while in the resistance ranges apply. That is, though on-line troubleshooting testing for continuity is described in this book, it is possible only on certain meters appropriately designated for use on live circuits in the continuity range. Do not assume that any DVM will safely perform resistance or continuity measurements on a live circuit unless specifically stated. ("Overload protected" means the meter has a fuse or internal circuit breaker. It does not mean the meter is designed to operate with a voltage on the conductors during resistance testing.)

The primary tests in which a VOM or DVM would be used in electrical troubleshooting work are as follows:

1. *Voltage value tests.* With the selector switch set on the appropriate (or higher) voltage range, the test leads are physically held against any two conductors while an AC or DC voltage value is read.

This test is concerned with an actual value; therefore the VOM scale (or DVM digits) is read with precision. An example would be a reading between the phase leads on a three-phase motor to determine the voltage imbalance (voltage difference) between phases. That test would be conducted by touching the leads to each of the conductor pairs and comparing the values. (For example, phase A-B might read 236 V, phase A-C might read 237 V, and phase B-C might read 232 V. You would know that the maximum imbalance was 5 V between phases A-C and B-C.)

2. *Voltage status tests.*   With the selector switch set on the appropriate (or higher) voltage range, the test leads are physically held against any two conductors to determine the presence or absence of a voltage. A specific voltage value is not the concern; rather the mere presence (or absence) of a voltage indicates a status. An example would be a test across the two secondary terminals of the electrical panel's control transformer to verify a voltage to the control circuit. (For example, if the leads are touched across the two terminals, a needle deflection to the right would indicate that control voltage is present. The absence of needle movement would indicate an open circuit in the control transformer or in the conductors feeding the control transformer.) A DVM is used in the same way, though the digital readout is watched to determine if the digits begin counting to a significant voltage value.

3. *Live circuit continuity tests.*   With the selector switch set on the appropriate (or higher) voltage range, the test leads are physically held against two points on a common (energized) conductor. If the circuit is unbroken between the two test points, the voltage reading will be zero (or a very low value if there is a slight voltage loss in the line). A zero voltage reading is an indication (though not an absolute verification) of continuity.

On the other hand, if the circuit is open between the two test points and the conductors are energized at both ends of the circuit, the needle of the VOM (or the DVM readout) will indicate a full line voltage. As an example, a ladder diagram line can be checked for continuity by touching the two leads to various points along the common conductor. A voltage reading would indicate an open circuit. [For example, if the circuit of line 22 was being tested for continuity (refer to Figure 5.5) the test leads could be placed on wires 14 and 15. A full-voltage reading would indicate that some part of that circuit was open (either the jumper connection between wires 14 and 135, cr16, or cr8).]

[There is a problem with false readings, which should be explained. A zero voltage reading may indicate continuity. However, a zero voltage will also be obtained if there are two open circuits in the same

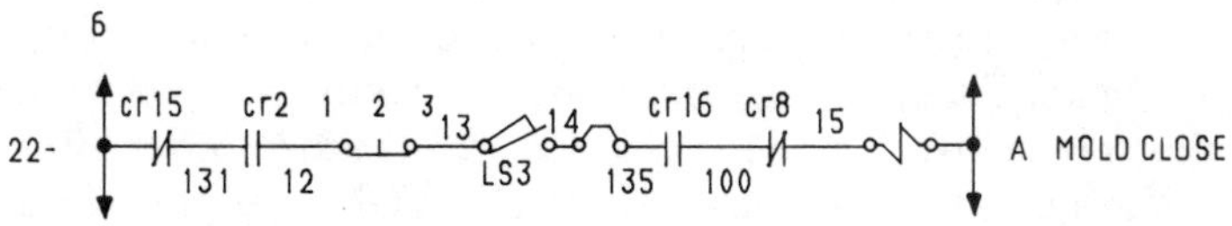

6

22-   cr15   cr2   1   2   3   13   14   cr16   cr8   15   A MOLD CLOSE
              131   12   LS3   135   100

Figure 5.5   Diagram line 22.

conductor. If there are any other open circuits outside of—but common to—the two points being tested, the voltage difference between the two points will still be the same. (For example, if the VOM leads are touched to wires 14 and 15, but LS3 is open, the voltage reading will be zero.) Thus, for an accurate test, it would be necessary to verify that there was a full potential voltage between *both* test points and the common grounded conductor. That is, if wires 14 and 15 indicate a zero voltage when the leads are touched to them, the leads must then be touched between wire 14 and ground and wire 15 and ground to verify that, in both cases, there is a full voltage. If in any of the two successive voltage tests there is not a full line voltage, the original continuity test is invalid. If LS3 were open, neither wire 14 nor 15 would show a voltage to ground, though the test between 14 and 15 would be zero. The advantage of on-line continuity testing (as described in the previous chapter) over voltage and continuity testing should be obvious. The continuity test is a measurement of the true state of the conductor, whereas the voltage test contends with other variables. There can be considerable time loss in verifying these additional variables.]

4. *Dead circuit resistance tests.*   After verifying that all parts of the circuit to be tested are deenergized, the meter is set on the lowest resistance range for continuity testing. (For most meters, the lowest range is designated as X1, which simply means that the number value on the ohm scale is multiplied by 1. Therefore, with the needle resting on 3, the value would be read as 3 Ω. If the selector we set on X10, the value would be 30 Ω for the same needle position. Similar values are indicated for each of the range multiplier designations. The designation K is often used for 1,000 and M is used for one million.) The test leads are physically touched to the conductor at the extreme ends of the section of conductor to be tested. A high value reading with no needle movement indicates infinity, or an open circuit. A low value reading with the needle at the right of the scale indicates continuity. As an example, the circuit of line 22 (Figure 5.5) could be tested using the VOM as a continuity tester. The X1 resistance scale would be used after calibrating the needle with the meter's zero adjustment thumb wheel. The meter can now be used to read continuity by touching the leads to any two test points on the conductor.

Because of the lack of power in the control circuit, all of the relay contacts have relaxed to their off position, which makes continuity testing more difficult. For that reason, an example will be given for a complete testing procedure for the entire line 22 (Figure 5.5). After verifying that the power is off, the leads of the VOM are placed on wire 6 and wire 131; this will verify the conductivity of the normally closed contact cr15. The next contact, cr2, cannot be tested, since it is open. Therefore, the leads will be placed on wires 12 and 135. This will verify the conductivity of switch S3, limit switch LS3 (which should be closed because the machine is set to cycle), and the jumper wire. The final continuity test would be between wire 100 and the common grounded conductor. This will verify the conductivity of cr8 and the mold-close solenoid A. (Relay contact cr8 could be tested on a dead circuit since it is a normally closed contact. On the other hand, cr16 was bypassed because it was open when the circuit was deenergized.)

If a break in continuity was discovered in the test completed so far, the cause can be isolated with further continuity tests. However, if the problem was not found, then there are still two additional relay contact areas which must be tested. They are the two normally open (NO) contacts. They can be tested in one of three ways. With the control circuit still in the off position, place the two lead probes on the relay contact terminals (which would be wires 131 and 12 for cr2 or wires 135 and 100 for cr16). Press a screwdriver against the mechanical relay push button—the VOM should now read continuity if the relay contact is operational. (Most control relays will have a button in a window that can be pressed to activate the relay.) The second way the contacts can be tested is to again set the VOM for a voltage reading, energize the control circuit, and set the machine in a stalled position so that line 22 should be functioning. With this setup, check for a voltage across either set of contact points as described under live circuit continuity tests).

The entire circuit can also be tested for continuity by jumping past the two NO relay contacts. Jumper wires would be placed from wires 131 to 12 and from wires 135 to 100. Electrically, the two relay circuits are completed, so that a continuity test can be taken on the entire circuit from wire 6 to wire 15. Aside from the safety consideration of using jumpers mentioned in Chapter 4, there is also the practical consideration that you may have bypassed the actual problem. That will, of course, be a clue as to what you need to further check, but it will add time to your troubleshooting procedure.

You should be able to see the speed and accuracy advantages inherent in on-line troubleshooting as compared with the troubleshooting procedures using a VOM or DVM. On-line troubleshooting can be summarized as having two areas of advantage:

1. You can test the entire circuit in its operational mode. Because the relays are electrically cycled, you do not need to use jumpers or bypass test points.

2. You are not introducing variables which are outside of the normal circuit operation. A relay contact may read continuity when you have closed it manually with a screwdriver, but you have not proven that it will not have high (or infinite) resistance when it is operating under load.

Troubleshooting with Specialized Continuity Testers

There are a number of continuity testers available for dead circuit testing. TIF Instrument supplies two such testers. Their Tic Tracer 300 has two leads which are used for continuity testing, in addition to the proximity conductor function which will be described in the next section. TIF also supplies a capacitor tester (model TIF660) which has a continuity function. Other suppliers have similar testers; most use probes or a combination of probes and alligator clip test leads.

These testers generally indicate continuity with an audible signal. They are used exactly like a VOM on the dead circuit resistance tests. The only difference is in the meter's audible signal response rather than needle (or digital display) movement.

The choice of an audible continuity tester response over a VOM (or DVM) for dead circuit continuity tests is largely a matter of preference. In some cases, however, there can be distinct advantages with the audible response. It is often easier to listen for a signal than it is to look at a meter. Many times these audible testers are more compact, and even though they lack greater application, they are generally less expensive.

The same precaution in testing only dead circuits applies to these meters as it does to VOMs and most DVMs. Unless specifically stated that the given tester is designed for live circuit testing, the circuit must be deenergized before any testing is done.

Troubleshooting with On-Line Continuity Testing

On-line continuity testing is a form of contact testing. That is, the meter's leads are in physical contact with the conductor under test. As was previously described, this means that the meter's circuit is common to the live conductor. From the previous discussion of VOM and standard DVM meters, it should be obvious that on-line continuity testing will require specialized test instruments which can be used on live circuits while they are in the resistance and continuity settings.

Available testing equipment

There are a number of meters from various suppliers which have the capability of live continuity testing. It is important, however, before using any meter for testing, that you read the material supplied with the instrument, and that you use it according to the supplier's recommendations. Generally speaking, the designation "overload protected" does not qualify an instrument for continuity testing on a live circuit. A designation indicating a maximum voltage (usually 250 V) for the resistance and continuity modes may allow on-line continuity testing. (It will generally show the symbols for continuity and ohms followed by "250 V max".)

Hioki supplies instruments which can be used for on-line continuity testing. The Pencil Hi Tester 3218 can be used for on-line testing as well as a full range of conventional voltage and resistance testing. Their Pencil testers are an asset to any electrician's toolbox. Their economically priced Card Hi Testers can also be used as continuity testers on a live circuit. (See Figure 5.6 for an illustration of Hioki's instruments.)

AWS supplies two instruments which also list a continuity function with a maximum 250 V allowable voltage on the line during continuity testing. However, they state that additional fuse protection must be used with their Electro-Probes for on-line continuity testing. (See

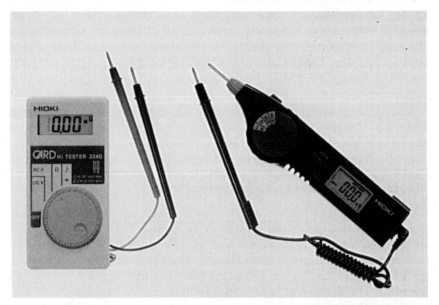

Figure 5.6 Two Hioki meters. The Card Hi Tester (left), and Pencil Hi Tester 3218 (right). (*Hioki-RCC, Inc.*)

the example in Figure 5.7.) They provide a manual ranging meter, Electro-Probe DM6592, and a fully autoranging meter, Electro-Probe DM6593. The fully automatic meter has the advantage of a clear tone for full continuity, and a periodic beep for higher-resistance conductivity. This distinction is valuable when the actual portion of the circuit under test is open even though there is feedback from other parts of the circuit. (All the other meters listed above make a distinction between a steady tone for full continuity, and a squawking tone when there is higher-resistance conductivity in other parts of the circuit.)

Greenlee BEHA Corporation supplies two test instruments which can safely test for continuity with up to 500 V on the line. The Unitest 575 voltage and continuity tester is a very versatile instrument for live circuit continuity testing. All functions are autoranging so that either continuity or voltage values are given. (The voltage values are given in fixed increments such as 12, 24, 120, 208, 277 rather than as actual values.) This is an extremely easy instrument to use for this type of testing since it will tell you that you have either continuity or voltage (a voltage value is an indication of an open circuit) without switching back and forth between ranges. Greenlee BEHA's Ohmvariator capacitor tester can also be used as a live circuit continuity tester and indicates the presence of an AC voltage as well. (The Ohmvariator has some very useful testing functions for capacitors, diodes, motor windings, and the like.) Of the two, however, the voltage and continuity tester Unitest 575 is better adapted to the test procedures described here. (Refer to Figure 5.8 for an example of these two instruments.)

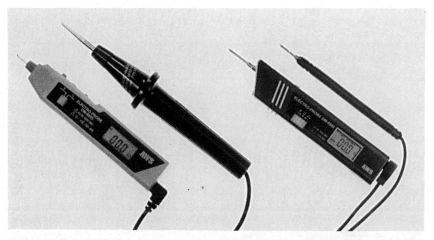

Figure 5.7 Two AWS (Sperry) instruments. The autoranging Electro-Probe model DM-6593 (shown with fuse-protected probe (left), and a manual ranging Electro-Probe model DM-6592 (right). (*Courtesy of A.W. Sperry Instruments, Inc.*)

(Because model specifications change, however, you must verify that the meter you are using—or purchasing—can, in fact, read continuity on a live circuit. Model numbers are given in this text for reference purposes only.)

Chapter 4 gave a complete description of the use of these meters in the troubleshooting examples. That information will not be repeated in this chapter.

The Hioki and AWS meters listed above have a full range of testing capabilities. With the exception of milliamperage ranges, they can perform all of the normal tests available on most VOMs or DVMs (though they have an upper voltage range limit of 500 V). The Pencil Hi Tester and Electro-Probe meters have the further advantage of allowing complete control with two hands (as against the necessity of holding a meter in addition to manipulating the two leads of a conventional unit). These meters also have the advantage of digital readouts. As with any digital readout, greater reading accuracy is possible.

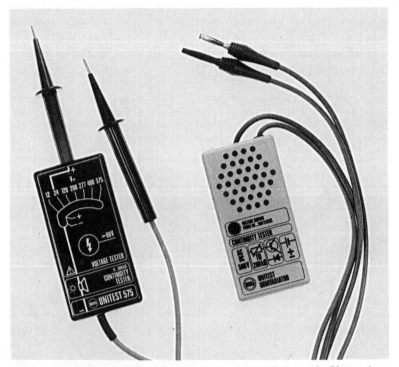

Figure 5.8 Both Greenlee BEHA's Unitest 575 (left) and Ohmvariator capacitor/continuity tester (right) can be used for continuity testing on live circuits. (*Courtesy Greenlee BEHA Corporation.*)

Testing Programmable Controller Circuits

New equipment is increasingly using programmable controllers (PCs) rather than relay logic circuits. In many cases, the external control switches, limit switches, and other make-and-break parts of the control circuit will be similar to conventional relay controlled circuits. However, you must practice extreme caution in testing these circuits (if, in fact, you test them at all with the methods described in this book).

A voltage applied across an open contact may energize the circuit of a programmable controller. Even the lowest current producing solid state meters may introduce enough current into the control circuit to energize an input port of a programmable controller. Therefore, if you are testing a circuit which is conductive to the input side of the PC, you run the risk of cycling a controlled portion of the equipment. In other parts of the book I have talked about the need to set equipment so that it can safely cycle when you are doing on-line troublshooting. With a PC, however, you may have an entirely different condition. You can actually *energize* an otherwise open circuit with your meter. Indiscriminate testing has a risk of doing great equipment damage to say nothing of the risk to personnel.

When a PC circuit is properly installed, the input ports (terminals) to the PC are fused so that your meter would not damage the actual programmable controller. (That is, if you want to risk your reputation—and pocket book—on someone else's installation of proper fuses!) You still introduce risk to sensors and other equipment when you indiscriminately apply unknown voltages from your meter to the very sensitive input and output equipment which is used on PC circuits.

Therefore, unless you are certain of what you are doing, do not try to use on-line troubleshooting techniques on programmable controller operated equipment.

Troubleshooting with On-Line Noncontact Testing

As mentioned earlier in this chapter, noncontact testing uses the electrical field of the conductor (generally of an AC circuit) as the source of energy for the meter's processing functions. The use of the clamp-on ammeter will be mentioned later in the book since there are some specialized troubleshooting techniques which depend on precise measurements of amperage. For now, however, I want you to discover a very useful electrical panel procedure which can be done with two novel instruments.

Specialized testing equipment

Both TIF Instrument's Tic Tracers and Greenlee BEHA's Volt Ticks (both companies provide several models) are capable of indicating a live AC conductor irrespective of load. The conductor does not need to be carrying a current in order to signal the presence of the voltage. Furthermore, it is done by proximity; there is no physical contact with the live circuit. (Refer to Figure 5.2 and Figure 5.8.)

In Figure 5.5 you have the diagram for the mold-close solenoid (solenoid A) of line 22. As you already know, any malfunction which leaves the circuit open will prevent the solenoid from cycling. In the on-line troubleshooting technique in the previous chapter, you set the machine so that it would stall when it came to the inoperative function. Now, referring to Figure 5.5, it is obvious that if relay contact cr16 were to fail, the mold solenoid would not function. Consequently, the purpose of troubleshooting is to find the last point on the conductor with a voltage. That point will be adjacent to the electrical component which is inoperative or open. Because you were told in the last example that the problem is with cr16, the last point on the conductor which will have a voltage will be the terminal screw of cr16 for wire 135.

Every troubleshooting technique using the ladder diagram to find open circuits is essentially using some form of electrical information to locate the final point of conductivity on that particular control wire. Consequently, voltages are measured from various points, or continuity is read to locate open circuits. The information is then used to extrapolate the location of the open circuit. The Tic Tracer or Volt Tick reads that information directly! (When I received the first of these instruments, I didn't believe it could really work. So I took a single insulated conductor about 3 feet long and plugged it into the hot side of a 120-V receptacle. Just a single open wire, so there was obviously no current draw. The tester—it would be true of either the Tic Tracer or the Volt Tick—sounded its buzzer right out to the end of the conductor and then gave the "open" beep when the probe went past the end. What more could I ask for in troubleshooting electrical problems in a panel? I can now find the end of a malfunctioning circuit!)

Both TIF Instrument and Greenlee BEHA supply noncontact testers which can be used to trace "hot" lines. (TIF supplies two models which can be used on 120-V control circuits, Tic Tracer 100 or Tic Tracer 300. Greenlee BEHA also supplies two models which would be used on control circuits, Volt Tick 10 or Volt Tick 2011.) All of these are precision instruments and can greatly aid you in your troubleshooting work. They are invaluable for locating hot lines, checking fuses, testing a component by checking the "in" and "out" leads, and many other tests where

Figure 5.9 BEHA Corporation supplies several models of their Volt Tick proximity tester. Model 2010 (shown) and model 2011 are similar; model 2011 has a dual range function for working in densely wired electrical panels. (*Courtesy Greenlee BEHA Corporation.*)

you want to determine if an insulated conductor is live. However, when you are doing on-line troubleshooting inside a crowded electrical panel, you must be aware of the instruments' limitations. Because these instruments are sensitive to the surrounding electrical field, the density of the field in a control panel makes it difficult (if not impossible) to isolate a single wire for testing unless special provision has been made on the instrument for this type of testing. (Generally, it is not possible to discriminate between wires closer than one-half inch apart. With many wires in the same vicinity, the distance grows to greater than one inch.)

Greenlee BEHA has solved the problem with a dual sensitivity model (Figure 5.9). Their Volt Tick 2011 can be used to identify a single conducting wire which is immediately adjacent to other live wires. I would recommend the model 2011 for any troubleshooting where you are working inside an electrical panel or where you need to distinguish between closely spaced wires. This model not only has a dual range capability, it can also be tuned for the desired response in either range. Because of the limitation of the other noncontact testers when used in an electrical panel, the testing example which follows uses a Greenlee BEHA Volt Tick 2011.

Actual testing

You are now going to troubleshoot line 22 from Figure 5.5. (You have already determined that solenoid A is not functioning.) You have stalled the machine so that solenoid A should close and everything has been left in the operational mode. You are now ready for the test.

Test 1. Verify the tester's operation. When held away from conductors, a periodic beep indicates the absence of a voltage. By holding the probe adjacent to a known hot wire, there should be a steady tone. Testing is done in the close quarters of an electrical panel with the tester in the lowest sensitivity range. Otherwise, the stray fields in the panel would cause a continuous tone irrespective of the absence of a voltage in an individual wire. Set the tester for the necessary sensitivity.

Test 2.   Arbitrarily select a midpoint on line 22 and test for a voltage. Hold the probe next to wire 14.

Purpose.   To verify the presence of a control voltage.

Test result.   Steady tone = control voltage. (You know the break in the circuit is beyond wire 14.)

Test 3.   Select a point between the solenoid and the last test; hold the tester's probe next to wire 15.

Purpose.   To verify the presence of a control voltage.

Test result.   Periodic beep = no control voltage. (You know the open circuit is between wire 14 and wire 15.)

Test 4.   Select a point between wires 14 and 15; test wire 100.

Purpose.   To verify the presence of a control voltage.

Test result.   Periodic beep = no control voltage. (You know the open circuit is in the jumper or cr16; the relay is the most likely location of an open circuit.)

Test 5.   Place the probe on both terminal screws of cr16.

Purpose.   To verify cr16 as being faulty.

Test result.   Steady tone on wire 135 of cr16; periodic beep on wire 100 of cr16. (You know the relay contact is open.)

It should be apparent that the troubleshooting sequence just demonstrated is extremely fast. It also has the safety advantage of testing conductors without physically touching any part of the circuit with conducting probes or leads.

The testing pattern for noncontact testing is the same as the one used earlier in the example of on-line troubleshooting given in Chapter 4. In both cases you divide the circuit and test it at a midpoint. Depending on the results, you subdivide the circuit into smaller sections until you isolate the break in the circuit. The difference, however, is that you are not testing for continuity with this noncontact test. Rather you are testing for the presence of a voltage on a line which indicates that the line is unbroken from the source to the point at which the meter is beeping.

There is an advantage with noncontact testing in that you are not using two meter leads as you would be with continuity testing. It is simpler to hold the nonconductive probe against a single conductor. In addition, you do not need to locate an open terminal for the testing since you can take the reading from an insulated wire. (It may save you the effort of removing a cover plate on a limit switch. If the switch is working, both wires leading to the switch would test as hot any place on the wire. If the switch is faulty, only one of the two wires would test as hot.)

Chapter Review

Advances in electronic test equipment technology have brought significant improvements in the speed and accuracy now possible to the maintenance electrician's troubleshooting procedures. The reduction of troubleshooting time will mean an increase in machine productivity. In order to achieve the full potential of the present electronic testing equipment, however, the procedures and methods used by the troubleshooting electrician will need to be updated to the capabilities of the equipment which is now available.

Electrical testing is generally done with either contact measurement or noncontact measurement techniques. In contact measurement, the leads of the test instrument are in physical contact with the live circuit under test. That is, the circuit of the test instrument is common with the live circuit. In noncontact measurement, the test instrument is sensitive to the electrical field of the conductor being tested; the circuit of the meter is isolated from the conductor it is testing.

The D'Arsonval moving-coil meter has been, until recently, the standard meter movement in most electrical measurement equipment. The moving-coil meter has a spiral spring-biased armature placed between two pole magnets. A properly calibrated coil will rotate linearly in response to a linear voltage applied to the armature terminals. The full voltage range of a D'Arsonval coil is generally less than 0.5 V. All voltage functions (AC or DC), resistance measurements, and current measurements can be read on an analog scale using a moving-coil meter when the appropriate resistance, rectification, and battery powered circuits are added.

The volt-ohmmeter (VOM) and digital voltmeter (DVM) are used in similar fashion in electrical troubleshooting. These meters are used for: (1) voltage value tests (where an actual voltage value is sought), (2) voltage status tests (where the mere presence or absence of a voltage is sought), (3) live circuit continuity tests (where the voltage ranges are used to indicate an unbroken conductor), and (4) dead circuit resistance tests (where the resistance ranges are used to measure continuity of deenergized conductors).

Because of recent advancements in the field of electronic testing equipment, two new testing procedures are now available to maintenance electrical troubleshooters. True continuity testing can now be done on live circuits, and field-sensitive, noncontact testing equipment is available which allows the tracing of an energized conductor requiring no electrical contact.

Chapter Questions

Thinking through the text

1. Define and explain contact testing.

2. Define and explain noncontact testing.

3. In what ways is a D'Arsonval moving-coil meter similar to a permanent magnet DC motor?

4. A voltage meter will show an AC or DC voltage as an effective voltage value. (A root-mean-square value.) How is the comparison value of AC and DC voltage derived?

5. What precautions are given when using a VOM for voltage or resistance testing?

6. Name and briefly describe the four types of tests for which a VOM is most frequently used in plant maintenance diagnosis.

7. What do the X1, and X10, X100 designations mean on a VOM's resistance ranges?

8. What does "overload protected" mean on a VOM or DVM?

9. Every troubleshooting technique using the ladder diagram is essentially using test information to locate the final point of conductivity. What test information is generally used? How is it obtained in the circuit?

Deepening your electrical understanding

10. The accuracy of readings made with a D'Arsonval moving-coil meter is dependent, in part, on the scale selection for a given test. Can you explain how to get the most accurate readings from this type of meter? Why, in your judgment, does the meter respond in this way? Can you give examples of various

kinds of testing conditions in which this accuracy either is, or is not, significant?

11. Four types of tests using the VOM are described for general plant maintenance diagnosis. In some cases, this will involve reading a value after the meter's needle has come to a steady position. In other cases, the mere swing of the needle (or lack of movement) is all that is significant. A DVM also goes through a counting-up sequence before the final value is displayed. For some tests, you will want to wait until you see the final value. In other tests, you do not need the final value but have all of the necessary information when the DVM begins counting. When using a DVM for each of these four tests, what do you need to see on the display? (That is, do you need to see a final value or merely verify that a count-up is taking place?) Give some examples of the meter values you would expect to see for different test conditions.

12. Select a circuit line from the ladder diagram and describe various troubleshooting procedures you would use for testing that particular circuit. Select various types of test instruments as described in the chapter to do your troubleshooting.

6

Collecting Information

In this chapter you will learn how to gather information which will make your troubleshooting faster and more effective. First, you will learn how to obtain information which will help you find an electrical malfunction. Secondly, you will learn how to use information to prevent future problems.

Stop, Look, and Listen

No better advice could be given for the first step in electrical troubleshooting. In my own experience in troubleshooting electrical production equipment, a significant percentage of the equipment failures are not electrical problems in the panel—they are something outside the panel which can often be seen with careful observation. Let me give you an example.

A plastic injection molding machine operator came to tell me that the machine would not cycle; after ejecting the last part it simply quit functioning. Had I started my troubleshooting in the panel, I would have found that solenoid A (mold close) on line 22 was not functioning. (Refer to Figure 4.1.) However, before assuming that it was an electrical problem, I did a quick visual check of the machine. The visual inspection revealed the problem! A flexible grease line had broken and fallen into the return path of the ejection system. As a result, the limit switch LS15 on line 36 (refer to Appendix A) was open. Since this limit switch controlled CR16, and CR16's contact is on line 22, I had found the problem.

Inspect the physical equipment

Each type of equipment will have its own set of checkpoints. Nonetheless, as you begin the process of troubleshooting, make an inspection of the physical equipment your first step unless there are clear indications otherwise. (If the motor is dead and the fused disconnect is smoking, you will be forgiven for checking that first rather than inspecting a safety gate which is ajar!) Of course, as you get to know the equipment, you will bypass many checks. If the motor is running and the control panel indicator lights are glowing, you know that the main power and the control power are operational—your first checks will not be in these areas. But get into the habit of looking knowledgeably at the physical equipment before you assume that the problem is caused by an electrical malfunction.

Sharpening your sense of observation will result in more than troubleshooting time savings after an actual failure. It is also an invaluable preventive maintenance and safety skill.

Many failures—electrical, mechanical, structural, etc.—give ample early warning signs for the observant maintenance person. Excessive heat or flashing around contacts, high noise levels, hot conduits or boxes, and many other sensory perceptions may be an indication that work is needed. If the warning signs are caught early enough, there may be significant savings in reduced equipment losses. (I will talk about replacing a compressor motor later in the chapter.) It is an interesting illustration at this point, however, because I heard the compressor motor thrashing itself to death. I was welding under a mezzanine where it was mounted. Though the welding was noisy, I sensed that something was wrong. The next time it started, I stopped to listen and decided I should go and have a look. I was on the way to the mezzanine when it actually burned out. The motor had undoubtedly been drawing excessive current for some time and the insulation was very likely in the final stages of breaking down. However, it was an interesting example of equipment signaling its need for attention. It went from a normal-sounding start cycle to complete failure in no more than four or five starts.

Good observation enhances safety

Safety is another area in which keen observation may be highly rewarded. As electricians, we are frequently around machinery and equipment which has high potential for injury to either personnel or the equipment itself. That is certainly true of the electrical part of the installation, and is usually the case with the mechanical and structural elements as well. Again, by being alert to abnormalities, we may well spot something which can be corrected before causing expensive damage. (Inasmuch as safety and observation are the topic, let's take this a step further. Having worked with a number of individuals on both ends of the safety-awareness spectrum, I believe I can make an important observation from the examples I have seen. It seems as though the "shop hazards" are more than just reckless. In many cases, these individuals seem to lack the ability to conceptualize—or imagine—how something could be dangerous. It may, in some cases, be a lack of knowledge; in other cases, a lack of thinking through the consequences. In contrast, the individuals who work safely do so because they have a sense of what might happen down the line if what in front of them is done incorrectly. The observation, then, is that true safety practice comes from the ability to visualize hazardous conditions before they occur. The truly safety conscious person is the one who is able to modify or prevent conditions before injury or damage takes place.)

Troubleshooting Sequence

Unless you have specific information which will more quickly isolate the problem area, I would suggest this type of sequence in most electrical troubleshooting problems:

1. *Get information from the operator(s).* This is an art! You will soon learn that if the machine was at fault, the answer to what happened will be, "I don't know, it just quit." On the other hand, if the operator was at fault, then you will get the answer to the same question as, "I don't know, it just quit." (You're sharp! You noticed the similarity of the two answers!) So, you will need to refine your questioning skills (taking into allowance both the machine and the operation). You will want to ask questions such as, "How was it running before it malfunctioned?" "Were there any unusual sounds (smells, machine sequences, etc.) when it was last running or when it quit?" "What positions were the switches in?" "What switches have been changed?" "Did you free any jammed parts or change anything?" "Was anything dropped (unplugged, bumped, etc.)?" Finally, if safety allows, you might want to ask the operator to cycle the equipment again. If you watch carefully, you may discover an operator-related problem (Figure 6.1).

You will need to evaluate the information you receive carefully. Not everything the operator tells you is necessarily correct. (The real problem may be that the operator assumed that a switch was in a certain position, or that the machine had completed a sequence.) Even so, do not make the mistake of discounting what the operator has to say. He or she has spent considerable time running that piece of equipment. The operator may not understand the technical reasons behind the machine's operation, but nonetheless, you will find that a good operator has an extremely well-developed awareness of when something is

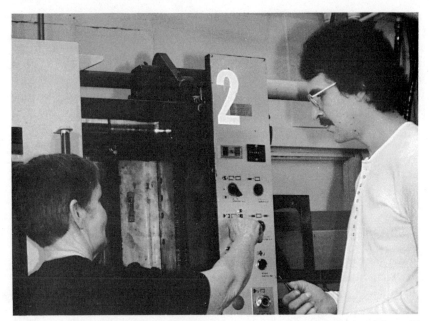

Figure 6.1   Before actually testing circuits, a careful troubleshooting electrician will obtain information from the machine operator.

malfunctioning on the equipment. So carefully think through what you have been told. Many times the operator's description will give you the necessary clues for quickly finding the problem.

(In my early troubleshooting days I learned that lesson the hard way. I was asked to troubleshoot a die-casting machine. An electrical company had spent the day on it and failed. When I arrived that night, I desperately wanted to succeed! I checked the machine from stem to stern and also failed—though this happened before I was using on-line troubleshooting. When I first arrived, the die-cast operator mentioned that a ladle of molten aluminum had been dumped on an exposed conduit. If I had been listening, he told me everything I needed to know. The electrician who followed me found a conduit full of shorted wires with melted insulation!)

If you are not familiar with a given machine, you will need to have the operator explain how to run the equipment. You may need to have an operator or setup person explain various equipment functions and settings to you. Don't skimp at this point. If you need to, swallow your pride and ask the questions. Asking the right questions will be the fastest way to get the equipment back on line. Your speed in getting equipment into production will be the basis on which you will be judged as a maintenance electrician.

2. *Examine the equipment.*   Unless you have good reason for suspecting a specific area, your first troubleshooting task is to make an overall inspection of the entire machine or piece of equipment. (Depending on the type of installation, this may include an overall evaluation of the entire plant's electrical system starting with the service panel.) You will want to look at anything that has limit switches, electrical safety switches or interlocks, proximity or sensor switches, and the like. Look carefully at those types of switches which are adjustable or subject to abuse (such as door switches); very often these switches will become loose and move out of operational range or will have become damaged. It will surprise you how many times you will find a limit switch on a door or cam that will "click" if you move the arm after the door or cam is supposedly in the activated position. You will also be looking for adjustment problems, jammed parts that will prevent electrical or mechanical functioning of the equipment, tripped circuit breakers or overloads, damaged cords or conduit, and anything else on that specific piece of equipment that would affect the electrical function. You will also want to look carefully at panel control settings (hand switches and time settings). Incorrect settings can shut machinery down just as effectively as electrical panel problems.

3. *Do preliminary power checks inside the panel.*   Your first check after getting inside the panel will be on your main power supplies. Depending on what functions you have lost, you will check the load side of the appropriate circuit breakers and/or fuses. You will then want to make certain that the control transformer (and its fuses) is supplying power to the control circuit.

4. *Study the ladder diagram.*   Your first step with the ladder diagram will be to isolate the function (or functions) which are inoperative. This will take you to some power device on the right-hand side of the diagram. However, before you actually begin your electrical testing, think through the significance of each component on the line in question. A limit or function switch on the ladder diagram may be a clue to something that you need to check on the machine. You may also find something on the diagram that raised questions as you were doing your preliminary check. You may find a timer, a disconnect circuit, an optional function switch, or any number of things that need further confirmation. Studying the ladder diagram can often solve the problem with no electrical testing necessary by showing you what must be operational in order for that circuit to function.

A note is in order at this point. The five steps of the troubleshooting sequence are given in a logical order. However, as you become experienced with on-line troubleshooting and the specific equipment you are servicing, you will be able to take short cuts. As a matter of fact, I do not always follow my own suggestions as I am giving them to you here. With experience, on-line troubleshooting is so fast that many times it is easier (and quicker) to do the checking from the panel rather than verifying that everything is in its operational setting on each part of the machine. If I suspect that something is wrong on the machine, I will certainly check it. If not, after a brief preliminary check, I may go directly to the panel and begin isolating sections of the ladder diagram. As you gain experience with troubleshooting, you, too, will develop a pattern which will give you the best speed.

Preventive Information

A teaching hospital places high value on pathology. An autopsy does no good for the deceased patient, but it may have great benefit for future patients. So, too, I think a good troubleshooting electrician is one who will take the time to figure out why something has failed. Actually taking time to do failed-equipment autopsies may prevent future problems.

The reasons behind electrical failures

Contrary to the feeling of the electrician in the example in the first chapter, electric motors don't "just burn out." They burn out for given (and usually preventable) reasons. The motor loss in the first chapter was a result of a faulty bleed valve—proper evaluation of why the overloads were tripping could have saved the motor, the motor control equipment, and the expense of the downtime while the compressor motor was being replaced. In order to have accomplished that, however, our friend the electrician would have needed the ability to evaluate available information rather than to merely replace parts.

So, why do motors burn out? There are many reasons. But unless you know the specific reason why the motor you are now replacing burned out, the replacement motor runs a high risk of an early failure also. In the first chapter example the compressor motor burned out because a bleeder valve malfunctioned. With three phase motors, the most common cause is phase imbalance. (A voltage difference of only 3.5% between the phases will increase the motor temperature by 25%. A 25% increase in temperature will greatly reduce the motor's service life.) Yet, in spite of the damaging effects of voltage imbalance, how frequently is phase voltage checked—and corrected—when replacing a motor?

Now, let me finish the story I started earlier in the chapter and tell you why I replaced the dead compressor motor I was describing.

The electrician who made the installation saved some money on a used fused disconnect. To get the fuses to work, fuse adaptors were used which didn't make good contact. High resistance between the fuse and fuse adapter took the motor out. I junked both the motor and the obsolete disconnect! Knowing why the motor had failed was mandatory if I expected the replacement motor to give satisfactory service. (Besides, let's have a little sense of self-preservation. If the motor I replaced were to fail again, I would look bad. On the other hand, if I took a little more care in scouting out the reasons why the first motor failed and I needed to replace some shoddy workmanship from the first job, the need of the additional cost would rightfully go against the first electrician's credibility.)

I read an account of a 150-hp motor that had been rewound twice in two weeks. (That was expensive!) It seems that rats liked the warm coils when the motor was shut down at night. Of course, they urinated on the coils and the moisture caused insulation shorts. Why didn't someone take the time to find out what had happened the first time the motor burned out? (The final solution was to cover the cooling passages with screen. The night guard—not an electrician—got credit for the solution.)

Not all examples come from motors by any means. Why do contactors or magnetic starters fail? Too often the answer is, "Who cares?—just replace it." I once did an autopsy on a NEMA 1 size contactor which had failed twice. I found that the aluminum shading coil was breaking because of metal fatigue. (The contactor was used for resistance heating and was cycling frequently.) A better grade of contactor with a brazed copper shading coil solved the failure problem. On another job, a contactor's coil had failed. After actually ordering the replacement coil, I was looking carefully at what I had assumed to be a good contactor. Then I discovered why the first coil had burned. A piece of the steel lamination on the moving coil was broken and had enough movement to periodically shift, leaving a large air gap. Of course, the coil current was excessive, and heat was the result. I changed the order to an entire contactor; had I replaced only the coil it would have eventually failed again.

Understanding why equipment fails

The intent of this brief chapter dealing with postmortem electrical equipment evaluation is not to tell you how to check for various faults. Rather, I want to encourage you as a troubleshooting electrician to get into the habit of thinking through the "why" of failure. It is true that the electrical equipment we deal with has a finite service life. Too often, however, electricians are replacing equipment which has failed well within its expected service life because it has been abused, or because other controllable factors have been ignored.

Try to understand *why* the equipment failed. Use your test equipment and make some measurements of the voltages and the current draw. Tear the old equipment apart before you throw it in the trash can. Finally, read technical literature which will give you the theory of that equipment's operation.

A plant maintenance electrician is not just a state-licensed part-substitution artist. The electrical trade needs electricians who are able to evaluate electrical equipment and make judgments which will improve both the economy of the plant and the reliability and safety of the equipment. Certainly, an electrician will replace parts. However, if you as an electrician are able to understand the causes of the failures and see the warning signs of impending failure, your contribution will be immeasurably greater.

Get into the habit of determining why equipment has failed. The end result will certainly be a better electrician. It should also have an immediate benefit in improving equipment reliability and service life.

Chapter Review

In this chapter, careful observation is emphasized as an important part of good troubleshooting practice. Unless specific failure areas are suspected, a complete examination of the physical equipment is the first electrical troubleshooting step. A continued habit of careful observation becomes a preventive maintenance and safety benefit; future failures or hazards may often be avoided when careful attention is given to the physical condition of the equipment.

In the absence of an indication of failure in a specific area, the following troubleshooting sequence is suggested:

1. *Get information from the operator(s).* Their experience with the machinery they are operating will often provide a short cut in isolating problem areas. Asking specific questions will help you to more accurately determine the cause of the machine's breakdown.

2. *Examine the equipment.* An overall inspection of the entire piece of equipment is the first on-site troubleshooting technique. Many problems which appear to be malfunctions in the electrical panel will, in fact, be switch or control problems needing correction on the machinery itself.

3. *Perform preliminary power checks inside the panel.* The first check inside the electrical panel will be the main power supplies and the control transformer supply.

4. *Study the ladder diagram.*   The ladder diagram is first used to isolate the inoperative function in the equipment. The diagram is
then used to pinpoint potential problem areas with switches or electrical control devices.

5. *Do the electrical testing.*   The ladder diagram is finally used to
move through a testing procedure of individual components or potential trouble areas within the inoperative circuit. Information is
also collected for preventive purposes. Understanding why equipment has failed may be an invaluable source of information for the
proper protection of the newly installed replacement equipment.
Determining why equipment has failed may identify other areas of
maintenance need.

Chapter Questions

Thinking through the text

1.   What kind of equipment failures can be observed from outside of the electrical panel?

2.   Can you give an example, either from the text or from your own work experience, of a nonelectrical (mechanical) failure which simulated an electrical
failure in the panel?

3.   Unless there are clear indications for a specific electrical problem, what
should be your first step in electrical troubleshooting?

4.   What are some possible early warning signs for future failure of electrical
equipment?

5.   How might safety be improved through careful observation of plant equipment?

6.   List the five steps of the troubleshooting sequence.

7.   How might examining failed equipment prevent future problems?

Deepening your electrical understanding

8.   Careful observation is an important aspect in effective plant maintenance
and safety. Can you give examples from your own work experience illustrat-
ing this principle? (If possible, give a positive example of good prevention that
was a result of awareness. Also give an example of the results of lack of
awareness and how it might have been improved.)

9.   After listing the five troubleshooting sequence steps, the author states
that there will often be times when your knowledge of equipment or condi-

tions in the plant will allow you to bypass many of these steps. Can you give an illustration of this kind of step-saving sequence from your own work experience? Can you explain why, in the example you chose, you were able to determine the steps you took? (That is, why did you eliminate certain steps?)

Practical On-Line
Troubleshooting

In this chapter you will see the entire on-line troubleshooting procedure used to solve an electrical control problem. This chapter will review and apply the information you have learned to this point by demonstrating a step-by-step solution to three typical control panel malfunctions.

Let's imagine that you are the plant maintenance supervisor for a plastics injection molding company. (Among your other qualifications, you are a highly skilled, state-licensed electrician.) You have just been paged by the plant production manager because there is a problem with machine #18. The information you are given is no more specific than "The machine is having a problem with the ejection and is stopping during operation." It is 9:17 A.M.

You walk past the tool room for your tools. You take a straight blade and a phillips screwdriver, and your test meter. (Those are all the tools you will probably need! You didn't pick up a wiring diagram because that is already taped to the inside of the electrical panel.)

Collecting Preliminary Information

By 9:18 A.M. you are standing by the machine. Your first step is to get information from the operator. Through careful questioning you find that the machine has been running this particular job for two and a half shifts, so you conclude that the malfunction is most likely an equipment failure rather than a setup fault. You also discover that the problem has been developing over a period of several weeks. (The problem has occurred at such infrequent intervals, however, that it was not noticeably affecting production. An operator discovered that by setting the machine in manual operation and ejecting the part with the push button, the machine would again function automatically. On this morning's shift, however, it has shut down twice and the production manager called you.)

Setting the machine to stall

After a quick visual survey of the operator's panel, you find that the main Control Switch has been turned to the manual setting. The machine is stationary, though the motor is running and the panel lights are lit. (Thus, you know the main power fuses, circuit breakers, and control transformer circuits are operational.) Because the machine is in the manual setting, you cannot proceed with stalled, on-line troubleshooting.

Since there are no apparent risks in running the machine, you ask the operator to put the machine back into production. You then explain to the operator that you want to be called immediately the next time the machine malfunctions. With a careful explanation of the need for doing so, you ask the operator to touch none of the controls or safety gates until you return.

By 9:22 A.M. the machine is back in operation. In other words, your technique so far has resulted in only 5 minutes of lost machine time. (Compare that with the electrician who will shut the machine down and make a pretext of "troubleshooting" before even knowing the possible area of the malfunction. That little charade may accomplish nothing and yet cost an initial 30 minutes or more of downtime.)

Collecting initial information

Now is the time to ferret out some information. Since you have a ladder diagram taped to the inside of the electrical panel, that will be your first stop. (You brought the screwdrivers so you could open the main panel.) As you begin to look at the ladder diagram (refer to Figure 7.1), you realize you need more information from the operator; the malfunction could have been in either the ejection circuits (which would be in the lines numbered 32 to 36) or in the mold-close circuit (which would be on line 22 mentioned earlier in conjunction with Figure 4.1). Further questioning of the operator gives you the information you need; the machine failed to eject after opening. (If it had failed to close after ejecting, it would be a problem on line 22.) Now you know that the problem is probably located on lines 32 to 36. (Refer to Figure 7.1.) Or, more precisely, you know that CR8 (or solenoid I or J) is probably not sequencing properly.

While studying the diagram you noticed several things in addition

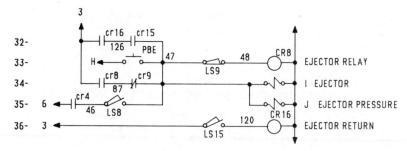

Figure 7.1 Diagram lines 32 through 36.

to the relays which should be checked in the circuit. First, you noticed that there are two limit switches in the circuit. (LS8 and LS9 are adjustment switches which are changed during setup. Since they are visible through the window on the operator's door, you can visually check these two switches while the machine is in operation to make certain that nothing is loose.) You also noticed that the count-up circuit (line 40 in Figure 7.2) is a part of the circuit for lines 32 to 36 and could potentially be a part of the problem. (Relay contact cr15 on line 32 is controlled by relay CR15 on lines 40 and 41.)

As you study the circuit, it becomes obvious why the ejector would work in manual even though it would not work in the automatic setting. Line 33 indicates that PBE (push button ejection) bypasses the entire relay-controlled circuit. (That is, PBE bypasses relay contacts cr16, cr15, cr8, and cr9.) It would be logical that an intermittent problem in the circuit could be reset by cycling the ejector relay. It also gives you an indication that the problem is not in the ejector relay (CR8) on line 33 or in either of the solenoids (ejector I on line 34 or ejector pressure J on line 35), since a failure in any of these devices would not allow the ejector to operate with PBE. The limit switch LS9 is also taken off the suspicion list for the same reason.

Since the machine is back in operation, there are some tests you can make to determine the machine's sequencing. As you study the diagram (refer to Figure 7.1), you realize that only one of the three lines

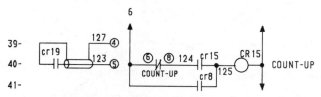

Figure 7.2 Diagram lines 39 through 41.

(32, 34, or 35) would normally be feeding CR8 at a given time. (There may be an overlap, however, when one line is switching to another.) Careful study of the diagram indicates that line 35 is the "initiate" circuit while lines 34 and 32 are "latching" circuits.

You can now do several preliminary tests to verify the function of each of these circuits. For the continuity or voltage (value) test, you will use a Greenlee BEHA Unitest 575 or Hioki's Pencil Hi Tester (or the equivalent AWS Electro-Probe meters). For the noncontact test, you will use Greenlee BEHA's Volt Tick model 2011 tester.

Preliminary On-Line Troubleshooting

For the illustrations in both this section and the actual on-line troubleshooting section, I am going to show you the procedure using both contact and noncontact testers. (These terms were defined in Chapter 5.) In the first case, you will be checking for continuity (or possibly a voltage value) on a live circuit with a contact tester. In the second case, you will be using a noncontact tester to verify the presence of a voltage.

Your first test using contact testers will be a voltage test; all other tests will be for continuity. (Bear in mind that the actual choice between a continuity or voltage test may be quite arbitrary. In many instances, similar results could be obtained with either. However, in some cases, there will be definite advantages to a continuity test under power, as was noted in Chapter 4. For that reason, this example will use continuity tests unless otherwise necessary.) Obviously, all tests with noncontact meters are, in effect, AC voltage field tests made on a single conductor. Refer back to Figure 7.1 as needed when performing these tests.

Test point 1

Contact (voltage) test: The meter leads are placed on wire 47 and the common grounded conductor.

Noncontact test: The probe is held next to wire 47.

Test purpose: To establish the presence (or absence) of a parallel control voltage to CR8, and solenoids I and J.

Meter indication (during each ejector cycle):

Contact (voltage) test: A voltage value is indicated.

Noncontact test: A steady tone is heard indicating the presence of a control voltage.

Test result: During each ejector cycle, a control voltage is observed for the duration of the ejection sequence. [*Note:* During normal operation of the machine, the meter can be read—or heard—while observing various relays' actions in the circuit. In this way you can easily verify the action of line 35 as the "initiate" part of the circuit; CR4 would momentarily close at the moment your meter first indicated a control voltage to CR8. However, the voltage would continue after CR4 dropped out. Similarly, watching each of the relays in the circuit would show you its function in the ejector cycle. It would be obvious that CR8 (through relay contact cr8) is the latching circuit and is broken when cr9 is opened.]

Test point 2

Contact (continuity) test: The meter leads are placed on wire 3 and wire 47.

Noncontact test: The probe is held next to wire 47.

Test purpose: To establish the sequence of the control circuit feeding CR8 and solenoids I and J. A single circuit will be indicated irrespective of which of the three lines (32, 34, or 35) is conducting.

Meter indication:

Contact (continuity) test: A steady tone will sound when the circuit is complete.

Noncontact test: A steady tone will sound when the circuit is complete. (*Note:* The Greenlee BEHA Unitest 575 meter is highly sensitive to grounding. If you hold the lead probe against the hot side of the circuit, your hand will offer enough resistance through the case of the meter unit to give a low-grade tone. Though you can accurately use the meter this way if you allow for the tone variation produced by your own body resistance, it is less confusing if you hold the tester so that the meter unit's probe is always held against the known hot wire, and the lead probe is used to test the unknown wires or contacts. Other manufacturers' meters may operate similarly. It is always a good procedure to do an initial check on both a known live and a known dead wire for comparison before you start the actual testing.)

Test result: Under normal cycle conditions, the test will indicate that there is a closed circuit between wires 32, 34, and 35 during the entire ejector cycle time.

By this time you have done almost all you need to do in the panel itself. However, a last series of tests might be worthwhile to give you a better understanding of each of the contact points in the circuit. By doing a continuity (or resistance) test across each relay contact (or limit switch), you can isolate that contact for observation during actual operation under load.

Test point 3

Contact (continuity or resistance) test: The meter leads are placed on any two wires separated by a single contact point (as for instance, wires 126 and 47 for relay contact cr15.) [*Note:* If you are using one of the meters capable of reading resistance (in ohms) with a voltage on the circuit, you can read the actual resistance across the closed contacts while they are under load. It is sometimes possible to spot a potential problem in this way since the resistance reading is often abnormally high prior to complete failure. However, carefully follow the manufacturer's recommendation concerning test duration. These meters have sensitive solid-state circuits which must dissipate heat. Even though some of these meters can tolerate a voltage on the line when they are used for a continuity or resistance test, they can only be used in this manner for short periods of time. Therefore, you will need to use a make-and-break technique for this type of testing, rather than continuously holding the meter across the hot line.]

Test purpose: To observe the electrical conductivity of the specific contact under test.

Meter indication:

Contact (continuity) test: A steady tone will sound when the circuit is complete.

Contact (resistance) test: The resistance in ohms will be indicated on the meter display. The reading should be zero. (A very low reading of several ohms may be permissible.)

Test results: Continuity or a specific resistance value can be established for individual contacts under load.

You have now completed all the work you can do in the panel until the machine malfunctions. Before leaving the machine, you do a visual inspection of the limit switches and the machine in general. Since everything is in order, there is little more that you can do until you are called. It is now 10:05 A.M. While the machine was running, you took some extra time to study the ladder diagram and use your meter.

This will save time later when you are called. You have been by the machine for more than 45 minutes, though actual machine downtime is still at 5 minutes.

Of course, you are going to get another call when the machine quits. Since I am trying to be as realistic as possible with this illustration, let's say that you are paged again at 11:50 A.M. (Which is realistic because 11:50 is 10 minutes before you were going to break for lunch!)

When you arrive at the machine you see that the operator followed your directions and left the machine stalled without touching any of the switches or safety doors. You can go immediately to the panel and begin your electrical testing.

On-Line Troubleshooting

As you begin the actual on-line troubleshooting, you are careful to follow all of the necessary safety precautions. In addition to personnel safety when working close to live electrical circuits, you have also verified that the machine could continue operation without danger to either personnel or itself. (Remember the caution regarding work on a stalled machine. You must determine that it could safely continue operation before you do any testing. If you electrically complete an intermittently open contact, the machine will continue to sequence.)

Reviewing the known information

Let's take a moment now and review the information you already possess concerning the machine malfunction and the subsequent direction you are going to go in your actual testing. Careful planning and appropriate use of information is an important part of the final time-saving aspect of on-line troubleshooting. Poor troubleshooting techniques are often characterized by a random, helter-skelter approach to all those mysterious wires in the electrical panel. For the problem which you are now troubleshooting, there is no need to test sections of the circuit which are not related to the ejector function. The failure is in the ejector system—so confine your testing to those circuits. (At the same time, you need to be careful that you do not overlook potential problems because they are not obviously a part of the ladder diagram line which you are testing. Many times you will find the problem to be in another circuit which is preventing the line you are testing from functioning. A good example would be a failure with the count-up function on lines 40 and 41. A failure on these lines most certainly could result in a problem on line 32 through counter relay contact cr15.) The portion of the ladder diagram you need for this testing procedure is found in Figure 7.2. This is what you now know about the machine problem:

1. All main and control power systems are operational (the motor is running and the panel lights and manual controls are operational). Therefore, you do not need to test fuses or circuit breakers.

2. The specific problem is in the ejector system. However, since the ejector will work on manual it is safe to assume that the problem is not in the ejector relay (CR8), limit switch LS9, or in either of thetwo hydraulic solenoid valves (the I ejector solenoid or the J ejector pressure solenoid).

3. The problem has been intermittent. That suggests that the malfunction will be at some contact point or wire terminal where manual cycling has restored continuity.

4. From your initial testing and study of the diagram, you understand the basic functions of the machine's circuit. Line 35 is a momentary "initiate" circuit. Line 34 is the latching (or holding) circuit. Line 32 maintains the circuit during counting (multiple cycle functions) and the return stroke.

5. As you begin your testing, the machine is stalled, which means that there is an open circuit which should normally be closed. You would expect to find that open-circuit condition on lines 32 to 35.

Continuing with the actual testing

Part of the reason you are a good electrician is due to the Sherlock Holmes in your blood. You have a hunch as to what the problem is going to be because of the preliminary testing you have already done. Your first step after opening the panel is to visually inspect the five relays in the ejector circuit. (Refer back to Figure 7.1 as necessary.) You find that CR16 is closed but the rest (CR15, CR8, CR9, and CR4) are open. You also know that there is an initiation (trigger) circuit on line 35. Since that is a momentary circuit, you know that you cannot test LS8 now. (You could test it by resetting the limit switches, but that would defeat your purpose in having the operator leave the machine untouched after it stalled. You will make those changes later only if you don't find the problem elsewhere, even though the initiation circuit is high on your list of circuit suspects.)

Your first hunch, however, is line 34. You think that CR8 is momentarily closing but not latching. The logical test is a continuity (or resistance) reading across cr9's normally closed (NC) contact.

Test point 4

Contact (continuity) test: The meter leads are placed on wire 87 and wire 47.

Noncontact test: Since cr8 is open, this test cannot be used.

Test purpose: To establish the presence (or absence) of continuity across relay contact cr9.

Meter indication:

Contact (continuity) test: Only a periodic beep is heard indicating the absence of continuity.

Contact (resistance) test: An infinity (0.00 MΩ) or very high ohm reading will show on the display.

Test result: Relay contact point cr9 is defective.

There is a high probability that you have found the reason the machine failed to eject, though you still need to confirm that cr9 is actually the cause of the problem. You could take a resistance reading across cr9 if you have not already done so. However, you will make your primary verification when you shut the machine down, turn off the power, and remove the inspection cover from the relay contact points.

To finish this illustration in grand style, that is exactly what you will do; you remove the inspection cover from relay 9. After taking the cover off, you find a badly damaged set of contact points which evidence arcing and heat. The contact spring has collapsed from the excessive heat.

Of course, you will now need to either replace the contacts (if they are available as such) or the entire relay. In either case, you have an inventory of spare parts in the toolroom, so the machine will not be down long.

How did you do on your troubleshooting time? It's now 12:04 P.M. which is not good for your lunch break because you still have a relay to repair (or replace). However, from the standpoint of effective troubleshooting, your time is phenomenal. The machine accrued only 19 minutes of downtime for your entire troubleshooting procedure! If you are as good at the repair as you were in the troubleshooting (and if you have the replacement contacts), you may still make lunch by 12:15 P.M.

This illustration is not totally unrealistic. Even though each problem you encounter will have its own set of difficulties, these kinds of successes should be routine. In a very similar type of problem, I located a loose wire on a relay terminal in less than 10 minutes of testing time. (It had been an intermittent problem for several days before I was informed of the situation. The operators were resetting a timer to get the machine back into operation.)

Special Setup Troubleshooting

On-line troubleshooting lends itself to another variation in the testing procedure. In many cases, you may need to troubleshoot an electrical function which does not stall the machine. A simple and fast way to do this is to reset the machine for a speed cycle and do the testing on that single function. (Of course, the machine could not be producing parts with this setup.)

If, for instance, the air system of lines 31 and 32 (Figure 7.3) was not functioning, you could quickly test it if the machine could be taken out of production and the timers changed. Since the air blast (which is merely used to blow against the part as an aid to ejection) is not necessary for the machine's continued cycle, you could set the machine to run without this function properly working. The testing can then be done on the defective circuit each time it should be (but is not) cycling.

Of course, you could do the testing by running the machine on a normal cycle setting. However, unless there is a need to keep the machine in production in spite of the failure of this system, the simplest way is to do a special troubleshooting setup. Assuming that the machine can be put into operation, you can set the limit switches and timers *so that material will not feed and the various timed intervals are only 1 to 2 seconds in duration.* Thus, when the machine is started, it will go immediately from sequence to sequence without any waiting periods. (That is, the timed material processing and cooling cycles have been eliminated.) The circuit in question can be quickly tested, because it is cycling every 10 seconds or less. This setup procedure can be used on many kinds of equipment where timed intervals are a part of the process. Each machine, of course, will have its own setup limitations.

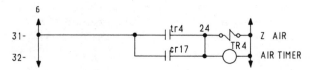

Figure 7.3   Diagram lines 31 and 32.

Assuming, then, that you can set the machine up for a short cycle, you would perform an on-line troubleshooting test on lines 31 and 32 as follows:

1. You will set all of the appropriate cycle timers and limit switches to their minimum (or zero) settings so that the machine will function for the minimum time (and in some cases, zero movement) in each sequence area. Before starting the machine, you must carefully check the entire setup for personnel and machine safety during operation.

2. In studying the electrical diagram, you know that if the problem is electrical, it will most likely be a failure of air solenoid Z or tr4 on line 31, or the air timer (TR4) or the relay contact (cr17) on line 32.

3. Your first test may be a voltage test from wire 24 (common to lines 31 and 32) to the common grounded connector. Since the solenoid and the timer are in parallel, the voltage reading would indicate the completed circuit for both devices.

   Contact (voltage) test: There is a brief audible or visual indication of a voltage during the first portion of the cycle interval.

   Noncontact test: There is a brief audible indication of a voltage during the first portion of the cycle interval.

   (*Note*: Again you have an initiate and a latching circuit. Relay contact cr17 is a momentary trigger circuit for the timer. Though the same circuit also puts a pulse on the air solenoid, it is too brief to actually cause the solenoid to function. However, when the timer is cycled, it latches tr4 on line 31 and holds the valve open until the timer times out. Thus, you may read two different voltages at the point you are now testing; either a constant voltage, if the circuit is fully functional, or a pulse voltage if cr17 is operational but the timer is not cycling. Since there was a brief voltage pulse, you can suspect the timer contact.)

4. Your most likely test is now across tr4. (Again, however, because tr4 is parallel with cr17, you will be measuring both functions simultaneously.)

   Contact (continuity) test: A brief audible tone is heard; the visual display momentarily shifts.

   Noncontact test: A brief audible tone is heard.

5. Though you will need to verify the problem with the timer (TR4), the malfunction is almost certainly in the timer drive or the timer contacts.

Evaluating the Procedures

With a little thought, it should be obvious that every troubleshooting problem is unique; therefore, there is not a standardized test procedure which satisfies every situation. Each of the three illustrations given in this book (the test on line 22 given in Chapter 4, and the two illustrations given in this chapter for the ejector malfunction and the air solenoid test) has differed from the others.

The first test on line 22 was done by moving from point to point on the circuit and testing for continuity. Since the entire line is a single circuit and is energized for the duration of the sequence, it was possible to do a simple continuity test while the machine was stalled. In other words, the test probes were simply touched to various points along the circuit until the open circuit was found.

On the other hand, the test of the ejection circuit in this chapter involved a number of contact points that were open at the time of testing. Because the lines being tested included an initiation as well as holding circuits, it was not possible to merely test across points on the lines in question looking for a single open circuit. Therefore, even though it was on-line troubleshooting, it required a combination of testing of the live circuit and an understanding of the function of the circuit so that the open contacts did not become an unnecessary source of confusion.

Finally, in the brief illustration of the air solenoid on line 31, you saw a test procedure which involved a machine setup especially for the troubleshooting test. In this last case, more direct on-line troubleshooting with a continuity test was again used.

On-line troubleshooting guidelines

From each of these three examples, there are some general guidelines which can be given for this testing approach:

1. Safe working habits must always be uppermost in the electrician's mind. This is true irrespective of the troubleshooting technique used. In on-line troubleshooting, safety precautions must include an awareness of working with live circuits and safety of personnel and equipment while either the machine is running or in the event that it cycles after being stalled.

2. There will be a great savings in troubleshooting time if an effort is

made to understand the circuit and to confine testing to the circuit areas in question. After studying the wiring diagram, you can determine where the problem is most likely to be found. Then conduct your testing so that you systematically move from the most likely to the least likely circuits.

3. You will achieve greater troubleshooting effectiveness when you properly use your test equipment. Take the time to determine the full range of testing capability of the meters you are using, and then take advantage of that potential. (Investing in adequate equipment is a necessary first step for the professional troubleshooter who wishes to do truly effective work.) Learn to use the best test for the particular need, whether that is a voltage test, a continuity test, a resistance test, or other tests which will be introduced later in the book.

4. Be aware of related circuits. Much confusion can enter into the troubleshooting process if you do not understand the significance of interrelated circuits. If a diagram line is found to be faulty, carefully check all other circuits that are represented on that line. (This is the advantage of continuity troubleshooting with an energized circuit. A continuity reading verifies the function of every controlled contact between the test points.)

5. Learn to test large sections. A single continuity test from the left side of a circuit line to the input side of the electrical device (or a voltage test from the grounded neutral to the input side of the electrical device) is all that is needed to verify that a circuit is functioning. If the electrical device is not functioning, begin the isolation process by subdividing the circuit into large segments for the preliminary testing. You will save much time by avoiding individual testing of each contact or switch.

6. Generally, most ladder diagram line testing will start with a confirmation of the electrical device or component on the right side of the diagram, and will then work toward the left of the diagram in the testing sequence.

7. Prudently make judgments as you work. For various reasons, there will be times when you cannot test every component in the circuit. Learn how to save time by passing over those areas which would be difficult to test. However, keep track of these short cuts so that your assumptions do not cause you to overlook electrical faults, forcing you to retest completed work.

Testing with multimeters (volt-ohmmeters and digital voltmeters) has not been covered in either this chapter or Chapter 4. Because these meters represent such an important part of the troubleshooting electrician's technique, Chapter 8 will deal specifically with testing procedures using these meters.

Chapter Review

On-line troubleshooting is most effectively done from a solid understanding of the equipment's normal function in comparison with its present malfunction. This preliminary information will come from studying the wiring diagram, from a general knowledge background of the equipment and electrical functions, and from specific questioning regarding the particular malfunction. A great deal of time can be saved in the actual troubleshooting process if the objectives of the troubleshooting are understood beforehand.

Inasmuch as each troubleshooting procedure will have its own unique demands, on-line troubleshooting cannot be reduced to a single formula. Most on-line troubleshooting, however, will fall into one of two formats.

1. The simplest format is one in which the testing is done across a single conductor which would normally be conductive (that is, a single-line circuit in which all of the switches and relay contacts are closed). In this format, on-line troubleshooting consists of verifying the conductivity of the circuit; any open point constitutes a fault in the circuit.

2. The second format is one in which the testing must allow for open conditions in the circuit during the time of testing, even though the equipment is in operation (or stalled, but under power). There may be a number of reasons why the circuit will be open at the time of the test. (The circuit may be a momentary or timed circuit, it may represent an auxiliary or overload function, or there may be other reasons as well.) In this format, on-line troubleshooting will require that certain parts of the circuit be bypassed or tested using other procedures.

On-line troubleshooting is, by definition, a test on an operating or live circuit. As such, the test procedure will most likely be conducted in one of three machine modes:

1. With the machine running in normal operation.

2. With the machine stalled (that is, where the machine is unable to continue to the next sequence), but where the controls remain set as though the machine would be in normal operation

3. With the machine speed cycling where the timers, limit switches,

etc., are set so that the machine can move from sequence to sequence at optimum speed. (This is called special setup troubleshooting.)

For on-line troubleshooting, you will be using either contact testing (which would include voltage tests or continuity and resistance tests with certain kinds of meters) or noncontact testing (which tests a single conductor for the presence of an AC voltage field).

Finally, there are general guidelines which will result in greater effectiveness and speed in your electrical troubleshooting. These would include an awareness of safety, understanding the electrical functions of the circuit you are testing, using your test equipment to its greatest efficiency, and conducting your test procedures so that you gain the greatest information from each individual test point.

Chapter Questions

Thinking through the text

1. Give examples of the information you might wish to obtain from a machine operator before starting a troubleshooting procedure.

2. What machine operating conditions would indicate that power supplies (fuses or circuit breakers) were functioning normally?

3. From the first illustration given in this chapter, the troubleshooter discovered by pressing push button PBE that, in all likelihood, the limit switch (LS9) on line 33 was operational. Why did the electrician come to that conclusion?

4. Aside from electrical hazards to personnel, what is the primary safety concern when doing on-line troubleshooting?

5. From the standpoint of the functions of the machine under test, what is the difference between on-line troubleshooting with normal machine settings and special setup troubleshooting?

6. Testing larger sections of a circuit will usually save troubleshooting time. Explain the meaning of testing larger sections. How will this reduce your troubleshooting time?

Deepening your electrical understanding

7. A ladder diagram may be read to explain the function of a machine under certain operating conditions. In this chapter, line 35 was labeled as a momentary trigger circuit. Can you use the complete diagram from Appendix A to explain how that information was obtained? (Pay particular attention to LS1 on line 46.)

8. In a manner similar to the question above, can you use the diagram in Appendix A to explain what would happen if a particular contact or limit switch failed? (You can either make the choice of a contact or limit switch yourself, or you might choose the normally closed contact in the count-up circuit found on line 40. The contact is not numbered as it is an internal contact in the counter found on line 37.)

9. Almost every test instrument has an advantage in certain test situations. Can you describe an electrical troubleshooting condition in which each of the following instruments would have a particular advantage: (1) A standard voltmeter. (2) A meter which can read either continuity or resistance with a voltage on the line. (3) A noncontact meter which can read a voltage field on a single conductor? (The advantages may be in ease or speed of use, safety, or any other criteria you choose.)

Troubleshooting with a Multimeter

In this chapter you will learn how the conventional multimeter (volt-ohmmeter or digital voltmeter) is used in industrial troubleshooting. Where possible, on-line (live-circuit) troubleshooting will be demonstrated in preference to resistance testing on a dead circuit. You will also learn how to do some specialized tests using multimeters.

The use of specialized, solid-state electrical equipment for troubleshooting is the primary emphasis of this book. Nonetheless, it would be a great disservice to the volt-ohmmeter (VOM) or digital voltmeter (DVM) to imply that they are not useful instruments for industrial electrical troubleshooting. The VOM and DVM are extremely helpful tools, as you will see in the following explanations and illustrations.

Before going further, however, you should briefly review the limitations and uses of these meters. (A more complete explanation of VOMs and DVMs was given in Chapter 5.)

General Precautions

When using a multimeter, there are two precautions necessary for the safety of the meter:

1. Most meters have a selector switch which is used to choose the test function performed by the meter. (The test functions usually include AC or DC volts, resistance, or amperage.) To avoid damage to the meter, it is important that the selector switch be set for the desired test before the leads are touched to the circuit. With the exception of autoranging meters (meters which can automatically adjust themselves to the circuit intensity) the function switch must

also be set to the appropriate (or a higher) range. (For example, many meters will have a 15-, a 60-, a 150-, and a 600-V range choice for AC voltage testing.) Attempting to test with the selector switch on the wrong function or on too low a range may permanently damage the meter (or blow a fuse if the meter is internally protected).

2. Unless otherwise specified by the manufacturer, multimeters can only be used for resistance testing on dead circuits. There may be exceptions with a few specialized DVMs; however, all VOMs (meters with a moving needle) must be used on a dead circuit when doing resistance testing.

The Basis of Multimeter Troubleshooting

The multimeter's most useful function in industrial troubleshooting is the indication of the presence or absence of a voltage. A voltage can be used to determine a live or functioning circuit, or it can be used to indicate an open condition along a conductor. Secondarily, the multimeter can be used for either continuity tests or actual measurement of resistance values when the circuit is dead. For a complete description of the use of the multimeter, refer to the information given in Chapter 5.

Troubleshooting with the Multimeter

In the last chapter, you were troubleshooting the ejector system. Let's go back and redo a part of that procedure with a multimeter. As you did before, you would start by collecting preliminary information. From the preliminary testing, you have already determined that the problem is with the ejector system on lines 32 through 36. Now, with the machine running, you will be testing to identify the circuit's functions. Refer to Figure 8.1 when doing the tests described in this section.

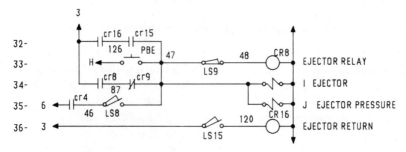

Figure 8.1   Diagram line numbers 32 to 36.

Voltage testing

Your first testing will be done on the meter's voltage ranges. You are attempting to find a point in the circuit at which the conductor is open.

Test point 1.   The meter leads are placed on wire 47 and the common grounded conductor.

Selector switch setting.   150 V AC.

Test purpose.   To determine the presence of a control voltage and the sequence of operation on CR8 and the two parallel hydraulic solenoids.

Meter indication.

VOM indication.   The needle swings to the right as the circuit is energized.

DVM indication.   The display counts up, indicating full line voltage as the circuit is energized.

Test results.   The circuit is verified as operational. A control voltage is indicated for the full duration of the ejection cycle.

Test point 2.   The meter leads are placed on wires 47 and 3 (Figure 8.1).

Selector switch setting.   150 V AC.

Test purpose.   This test will establish the sequence of the control circuit feeding CR8 and solenoids I and J. A single circuit will be indicated irrespective of which of the three lines (32, 34, or 35) is conducting.

Meter indication

VOM indication.   The needle will indicate 120 V when the combined circuits of lines 32, 34, and 35 are open and LS9 is closed. When the circuit is energized, the needle will swing toward 0 V.

DVM indication.   The display will indicate 120 V when the combined circuits of lines 32, 34, and 35 are open and LS9 is closed. When the circuit is energized, the display will count down toward zero.

(*Note:* When you are using a multimeter to check a live circuit for conductivity, you must read the information correctly. As in the example above, if you are reading an open area on a live circuit, the meter will show full line voltage. When the circuit is closed, the voltage difference between the two points should drop to zero.[1] The difficulty, however, is in distinguishing between a closed contact and a deenergized circuit. For example, if you are reading across wires 3 and 47, you will get a zero reading irrespective of the conductivity of the wires if LS9 is open. Thus, if you have a zero reading, it is necessary to verify the control voltage by testing between wire 3 and ground. A zero voltage between wires 3 and 47 and a 120-V reading between wire 3 and ground indicates that the circuit between wires 3 and 47 is conductive.)

Test results. Under normal cycle conditions, the voltage drops to zero during the entire ejector cycle time. The test indicates that there is a closed circuit on line 32, 34, or 35 during the entire ejector cycle time.

In the illustration from the last chapter, you did some additional testing while the machine was running. Similar preliminary testing could be done with a multimeter as well, though I won't take the time to go through each of those steps here.

On-line testing of a stalled machine

After the machine stalls, you will again start your on-line testing procedure. As suggested in the previous discussion, you suspect that cr9 on line 34 is failing. That is again how you will conduct your multimeter testing.

Test point 3. The meter leads are placed on wires 87 and 47 (Figure 8.1).

Selector switch setting. 150 V AC.

Test purpose. To verify that the normally closed (NC) relay contact cr9 on line 34 is conductive.

---

[1] The presence of a voltage less than the control voltage may be an indication of a high-resistance contact. If, for example, you were reading across cr9 on line 34 while it was under load and your meter indicated from 2 to 5 V, you would have an indication that the contact was failing. The voltage loss across a closed contact should be less than what most meters would readily indicate. Your multimeter will therefore indicate one of three things when you are reading across a contact: (1) A full control voltage reading indicates that the contact is open. (2) A zero voltage indicates that either the contact is closed or that the part of the circuit which you are testing is dead. (3) A voltage substantially lower than the control voltage indicates that the contact has high resistance and is failing.

Meter indication

VOM indication.   120 V AC.

DVM indication.   120 V AC.

Test results.   Relay contact cr9 has failed.

The presence of a voltage indicates that there is an open conductor at cr9. The meter is reading a voltage on two conductor ends (wires 87 and 47). If cr9 is open (but all other contacts on the line are closed), then all contacts including the electrical output devices (the wire-wound coils in CR8, solenoid I, and solenoid J) act as conductors. Rather than having a voltage drop across the electrical output devices as it should, the full voltage drop is across the open part of the circuit. For this reason, the open part of a circuit will always read full line voltage if the rest of the circuit is complete.

Off-line resistance testing

At this point, you could verify your findings with resistance tests. You will need to shut the machine down for your test since a resistance test with a standard multimeter must be done on a dead circuit. However, since cr9 is normally closed (NC), this will not alter the relay contact positions. (You could not do a resistance test on a normally open contact with a standard multimeter, since deenergizing the circuit for the test would open the relay. You could, of course, deenergize the circuit and manually close the relay, but that could alter the conditions of an intermittent problem.)

Your first step is to deenergize the machine. This would most likely be done by tripping the main circuit breaker. A wise precaution before using your multimeter as a resistance meter would be to measure for a voltage between ground and both wires 47 and 87. If there is no indication of voltage, you can proceed with your testing by setting your meter on the X1 resistance range.

Test point 4.   The meter leads are placed on wires 47 and 87 (Figure 8.1).

Selector switch setting.   The meter is set on the X1 resistance range.

Test purpose.   To test the resistance (measured in ohms) across the NC contacts cr9.

Meter indication.

VOM indication.   The needle indicates infinity (∞) or a very high resistance value.

DVM indication.   The display indicates infinity (0.00 MΩ) or a very high resistance value.[2]

Test results.   The NC relay contact cr9 is defective.

As you can see from the example you just completed, the mutimeter (VOM or DVM) can be effectively used for industrial electrical troubleshooting. Even though it cannot be used for continuity testing in its resistance ranges on live circuits, it can perform many of the tests described as on-line troubleshooting.

Specialized Multimeter Testing

In the following sections, you will see some testing procedures which go beyond the circuit of the ladder diagram. These tests will be done with a multimeter. (In Chapter 9 you will see some additional testing procedures which will be done with other specialized instruments.)

In many cases, absolute electrical values are not the objective of the multimeter testing done in industrial electrical work. If, for instance, you are measuring the resistance of each of the three windings in a three-phase motor, it is probably insignificant if the value is 3 or 7 Ω. What is significant is that there is a reading indicating a complete circuit with no reading to ground. The same is true of most voltage readings. With the exception, for example, of reading absolute voltage values to compare phase balance, most voltage readings done with a multimeter in industrial electrical work are done for the purpose of determining the presence or absence of an approximate voltage. With that in mind, there are a number of specific troubleshooting techniques which use the multimeter.

Multimeter resistance testing

The following tests can be made with a multimeter on the resistance settings. Consequently, all of these tests are done on dead circuits. (It will not be repeated for each section, but it goes without saying that the first test would be a verification that the circuit is dead, both as a safety precaution for personnel and as a prerequisite for resistance measurement with a multimeter. Verification of a dead circuit is done

---

[2] Correctly reading a DVM value will take a little practice. Several things make that the case. First, there is little standardization of readout symbols; each manufacturer will use what best suits its purposes. Second, with autoranging meters, such values as infinity (∞) will be designated with existing characters and decimals. Thus, infinity may be indicated as a function of megohms (0.00 MΩ) or even as a combination with the half-digit function displayed as (1.00 MΩ). You will need to familiarize yourself with your own meter's symbols.

with a voltage range higher than the known voltage of the system under test.)

Most resistance testing for industrial electrical work is not concerned with specific resistance values, but is rather looking for the presence or absence of a resistance which would be significant for that particular test. In other words, a test between a conductor and ground should show no value on the meter's lower resistance scales. Infinity (no resistance) would be an acceptable test result, whereas any significant resistance value would indicate a short circuit. A test of a magnetic starter coil would not be concerned with the actual ohm value (it could be as high as 200 Ω or as low as 20 Ω depending on the voltage rating of the coil), as long as it showed continuity. For this reason, most resistance testing in industrial work will be on the X1 resistance range. (The exception to an almost exclusive use of the X1 range would be in insulation testing, though that is more accurately done with megohmmeters which will be discussed in the next chapter.)

Phase-to-phase and phase-to-ground testing. The multimeter is often used for short-circuit testing between two phases (hot legs) or a phase leg and ground. For example, if you were testing a remotely located three-phase motor which was tripping its circuit breaker, it is possible that you would want to test for shorts between lines (phase-to-phase) or for shorts to ground (phase-to-ground). For the phase-to-phase test you would need to isolate each of the lines. Since there is a circuit breaker at the main panel area and a disconnect within sight of the motor, you can open both the circuit breaker and the disconnect and the lines will be isolated. To test for a phase-to-phase short, you will use your multimeter to test between phase A and B, between phase B and C, and between phase A and C. Using the X1 range on the meter, you would be looking for any needle movement as an indication of a short between the conductors.

Phase-to-ground is an easier test because you do not need to isolate the leads. (Obviously, however, you do need to disconnect the power.) For the same remote location motor, you would test between phase A and ground, phase B and ground, and phase C and ground. If there was no needle movement in any of these three tests, you would conclude that the motor (or its feeder circuits) was not shorted to ground.

If you understand how the multimeter was used to test the feeder lines for phase-to-phase or phase-to-ground shorts, you will be able to apply that same testing procedure to many other pieces of electrical equipment. Motors and transformers are often tested for shorts in the same way. The phase-to-ground is again the simplest test. You would test between any line lead and the motor frame; any significant meter reading would indicate a short. To test for phase-to-phase shorts, you will need to isolate each set of windings and test the leads between any two sets of coils. Again, the absence of meter movement is an indication that there are no short circuits. (In this case, you would want to use higher resistance ranges on your meter. However, with a standard multimeter, the lower ranges will indicate a reading with a shorted motor, whereas the higher ranges may not indicate a fault even if the motor insulation is breaking down just prior to complete failure.)

Transformer testing is done in much the same way as the motor illustration above. With an isolation transformer (a transformer in which the primary and secondary are separate windings) there should be no resistance reading between the high (primary) and low (secondary) sides of the transformer. Similarly, there should be no reading between any of the leads and the transformer case. (The exception would be if the transformer is used as a control transformer with a grounded conductor and is still in the circuit. Then one leg of the secondary circuit is grounded. A system ground may also be common to one side of the primary, which would also give a reading. However, in both cases, if the leads are disconnected from the transformer, there should be no resistance between ground and any lead.)

Continuity testing.   Resistance is a function of a completed circuit. For this reason, the multimeter's resistance ranges are ideal for verifying electrical circuits. The simplest example would be a magnetic motor starter coil. In the case of a nonfunctioning magnetic starter, you would need to verify the condition of the coil. Taking a reading across the coil on the X1 resistance range would indicate infinity (for an open coil) or resistance (for a serviceable coil). The resistance value is of little significance; you are merely testing to see if it is open or a completed circuit.

Many similar tests will use the resistance settings on the multimeter. All of the electrical components on the right side of the ladder diagram may be tested in this way. A relay coil, a hydraulic solenoid valve, a timer motor, or an indicator light would all indicate resistance if the circuit was complete, and infinity if the circuit was open. Ground short tests can also be made by testing between a power lead and ground.

Similarly, the ohmmeter can be used to verify switches. The meter leads can be placed across switch terminals to verify that the switch is functioning.

When you are testing resistance with an ohmmeter, you must be certain that the circuit you are testing is isolated. (The component being tested cannot be in parallel with any other closed circuit.) Your meter will measure any resistance which is in the circuit. For example, if two relays are connected in parallel (refer to CR17 and CR19 on lines 38 and 39 in Appendix A) you will obtain a reading whether both or only one coil is serviceable. Consequently, if you are attempting to test a coil which is normally in parallel with another, you will need to disconnect one of the leads to isolate the coil before doing the test.

There is a short cut, however, that can sometimes save you the time of isolating components on a parallel circuit. Measure a similar component in another part of the circuit—such as a relay coil—for its resistance value. Since the value of parallel resistance is less than the value of a single resistor, a resistance value less than that of a single, similar component indicates that both components in the parallel circuit are functional. (If the two resistances are of equal value the combined value will be half.) For example, if you measured another similar relay coil and found its value to be 100 Ω, the two series coils (CR17 and CR19) in the illustration would read 50 Ω if both were functional. If you obtained a value of 100 Ω, you would know that one of the coils was open.

Lead or conductor identification.   An obvious use of the multimeter is for lead or conductor identification. For example, if you have a stepdown transformer (with a 240-V primary and a 120-V secondary) which has four leads but no marking, you could identify the lead sets (but not winding function) with your multimeter. You would test between one lead and any of the remaining three. When the meter showed a resistance value, you would have identified the two leads to one coil. The remaining two leads would then test as the second coil.

Frequently, when testing in an electrical panel, numbered markers will be missing from wire ends. If, for instance, you know that wire 126 goes between relays CR15 and CR16, but the markers are missing from three of the wires leading to CR16, identification is simple. You will set one meter lead on wire 126 on CR15 and subsequently touch the second lead to each of the unmarked wires on CR16. When the meter indicates a reading, the unmarked wire 126 has been located.

Capacitor testing.   Though there are specialized capacitor testers, the multimeter can do a satisfactory job identifying shorted capacitors. (Before testing any capacitor, however, short the leads. Electrolytic capacitors can hold high charges which could damage a meter.) The first test will determine if the capacitor is shorted. A good capacitor should show an infinite meter reading when the test leads are touched to the capacitor terminals, whereas a shorted capacitor will show a low-value resistance.

Another interesting test for electrolytic capacitors gives an indication of their capacitive function. You must use a VOM for the test.

Start the test with the meter on the X1 range—higher resistance ranges give greater needle deflection, which may exceed the scale range of the meter. Place the test leads on the capacitor terminals; the needle will slightly rise and then fall. (You are actually charging the capacitor with the meter's battery.) Now, reverse the leads and watch the needle. The needle should swing sharply to the right and then slowly fall as the capacitor discharges. If the needle does not swing, the capacitor is leaking internally. If you do not obtain satisfactory readings, you may need to use higher resistance ranges on the meter.

Diode testing.   A multimeter can be used for a number of solid-state tests. However, for the electrician in industrial electrical work, diodes will be the component most frequently checked. A properly functioning diode will block the current in one direction while allowing it to pass in the other. Thus, for the first test, the meter leads are placed across the two diode terminals. The meter should indicate either a very high or a very low resistance value. By reversing the leads, the opposite (either low or high) reading should be indicated. A good diode will indicate a low resistance in one direction and a high resistance in the other. A faulty diode will most often indicate a low resistance in both directions, though a high resistance in both directions is also possible.

One caution should be mentioned regarding multimeters and solid-state equipment. Many solid-state circuits can be damaged by even the low current output of a moving-coil VOM. A VOM should never be used on circuit boards with integrated circuit chips or other low-power solid-state devices. Generally, a DVM (which has a much lower current output) can be used for this type of testing, though it is your responsibility to determine circuit safety before continuing with any testing.

Power testing with a multimeter

It would be impossible to cover the subject of power calculation and testing to any degree of adequacy in the limited space available. Yet it is worthwhile to give you several illustrations of what you can do in power testing with simple hand-held meters. A multimeter and a clamp-on ammeter can get you started with power testing.

Efficiency.   Electric motors have both mechanical (bearing and windage) and electrical (copper) losses. Therefore, the mechanical output divided by the input and multiplied by 100 will give a motor's power efficiency in percentage figures. For the purpose of calculation, remember that 1 hp equals 746 W.

$$\% \text{ efficiency} = \frac{\text{output}}{\text{input}} \times 100$$

Example 1: You need to figure the efficiency of a 1-hp motor which is operating in your plant. You simultaneously measure the voltage with a multimeter and the current with a clamp-on ammeter. The voltage reads 220 V, and the current is 6 A. What is the efficiency of the motor?

$$\frac{746}{220 \times 6} \times 100 = \frac{74.600}{1.320} = 57\%$$

Example 2: The name tag on another motor lists it at 50 hp. Your clamp-on ammeter reads 93 A and your multimeter reads 480 V. What is the efficiency of the motor?

$$\frac{50 \times 746}{93 \times 480} = \frac{37.300}{44.640} = 84\%$$

Horsepower. The formula for three-phase horsepower is

$$\frac{1.73 \times I \times E \times \text{ef} \times \text{PF}}{746}$$

where 1.73 = three-phase power
I = current in amperes
E = voltage
ef = motor efficiency
PF = power factor

Example 3: What is the actual horsepower of a three-phase motor which is drawing 51 A at 460 V? You obtained the voltage and amperage information with your multimeter and clamp-on ammeter. According to the manufacturer's information, this particular motor should run at approximately 94 percent efficiency. Finally, you estimate from information you already possess that your plant is running at a power factor of 80 percent.

$$\frac{1.73 \times 51 \times 460 \times 0.94 \times 0.80}{746} = \frac{30,520.5}{746} = 40.9 \text{ hp}$$

Obviously, the multimeter can provide information for any calculation where voltage and resistance values are required. In conjunction with a clamp-on ammeter, the necessary information for many shop calculations can be acquired. (Remember, however, that cold and hot values for the same resistance may differ greatly. In most cases, the only reliable resistance value would be one obtained under load, which was explained in Chapter 5. Resistance values can also be calculated from the current draw as measured by the ammeter. In the same way, impedance—which is the sum of the resistance, inductance, and capacitance in an AC circuit—cannot be measured as a single resistance value.)

A table of useful formulas is given in Appendix C.

Chapter Review

In spite of the availability of sophisticated solid-state test equipment, the multimeter [either a moving-coil volt-ohmmeter (VOM) or a solid-state digital voltmeter (DVM)] continues to be a very useful test instrument for the industrial electrician. For effective and safe operation, however, the multimeter must be properly used. There are two essential precautions when using any multimeter:

1. The multimeter selector switch must be set for the correct test function and range before starting any circuit testing.

2. All resistance testing must be done on deenergized circuits.

The multimeter's most frequent testing function in industrial electrical work is the indication of the presence or absence of a voltage. The voltage test can be used to verify the conductive state of the circuit. Secondarily, the resistance-testing capabilities of the multimeter can be used for testing the continuity of a deenergized circuit.

In many instances, the multimeter is used to merely indicate the presence of a voltage or resistance; the actual value of that voltage or resistance is inconsequential to the purpose of the test.

The multimeter can be effectively used for the following resistance tests:

1. Phase-to-phase and phase-to-ground testing for the purpose of locating short circuits.

2. Continuity testing for the purpose of verifying completed circuits in electrical wiring or electrical devices.

3. Lead or conductor identification for the purpose of labeling lead sets (pairs).

4. Capacitor testing for the purpose of identifying shorted or otherwise faulty capacitors.

5. Diode and other solid-state device testing.

The chapter concluded with a brief introduction to the use of a multimeter (often in conjunction with a clamp-on ammeter) for power testing. Such values as electric motor efficiency and horsepower can be determined from the readings of hand-held meters.

Chapter Questions

Thinking through the text

1. What two areas are mentioned as necessary meter safety precautions when using a standard multimeter?

2. During a conductivity test on a live circuit, what will the meter indicate across an open contact in the circuit?

3. During the same conductivity test on a live circuit, under what two conditions will the meter read zero volts?

4. What would a low-resistance phase-to-phase test on isolated conductors indicate? What would a low-resistance phase-to-ground test indicate?

5. Why is the indication of a resistance value a satisfactory test for continuity?

6. When testing a diode with a multimeter, the leads are reversed and two readings are taken. Why does a high and a low resistance reading (after the leads are reversed) indicate a good diode?

7. What losses reduce the efficiency of an electric motor?

Deepening your electrical understanding

8. It is emphasized several times in the chapter that a multimeter test may not require the reading of an actual voltage (or resistance) value. Can you give examples in which both sets of conditions are true; that is, an example where you will need to know a precise voltage and an example where meter movement is ample?

9. One of the difficulties of using a multimeter for on-line troubleshooting is the possibility of zero voltage readings for completely opposite circuit conditions. What are those conditions and how do you use the multimeter to verify the accuracy of the test?

10. Though resistance continuity testing is usually done without a need for knowing the actual resistance values, this is not always the case. For example, you may expect to see a value of 100 Ω or more across a relay coil. A relay contact should indicate close to 0 Ω. In both cases, a resistance value of infinity indicates that the circuit is open. However, what might you assume—and why—in the case of a higher-than-normal resistance value across the contacts? What might you assume—and why—in the case of a lower-than-normal resistance value across an isolated relay coil?

11.   A procedure was described in which you could identify the lead pairs (but not whether they were the primary or the secondary) of a stepdown transformer which had four unmarked leads. How could you go a step further and safely identify the primary and the secondary coils of this 240/120 V stepdown transformer? All you will need is a multimeter and a 120 V AC power source.

12.   If you are working in an industrial setting (or have bench equipment in an electrical classroom) can you calculate actual motor efficiencies or horsepowers from the formulas given in the chapter?

Specialized Tests and Equipment

*In this chapter you will learn how to do a variety of
specialized tests which are designed to reduce
your troubleshooting time. In many cases, these
tests will rely on specific types of testing equipment.
Both the testing procedures and the required
equipment will be fully explained.*

New Troubleshooting Possibilities

Increasing your electrical troubleshooting speed has been the emphasis of this book. That has been achieved to this point by an introduction of both new test equipment and testing procedures. The testing procedures thus far, however, have closely paralleled conventional testing in the sense that similar test points (relay and switch terminals, for example) are used. (Nonetheless, on-line troubleshooting greatly differs from conventional troubleshooting in that it utilizes continuity measurements with the control voltage on the line.)

In this chapter on-line troubleshooting will be taken a step further. You will be shown testing techniques which are possible because of the solid-state equipment which is presently available. Troubleshooting accuracy and safety are in no way compromised—they are often enhanced. Through a careful use of troubleshooting techniques—in conjunction with some truly fine test instruments—you will find ways to dramatically reduce the amount of time spent in troubleshooting motors, electrical controls, and other industrial electrical equipment.

Test instruments you will be using

Surprisingly, this chapter is not a covert attempt at encouraging troubleshooting electricians to mortgage their home for test instrument purchases. Most (though not all) of the equipment described in this chapter is within the budget expectations of any electrician interested in making a prudent investment in professional tools. To give you a very general idea of price range, I have compared the average union journeyman's hourly wage with the price of several of these instruments. The most expensive instruments would be the megohmmeters. They would require approximately 25 hours' wages (discounting withholdings) for the best of these meters. On the other hand, the highest-quality digital clamp-on ammeter would require only about half that amount of time. At the low end of the price scale, some of the equipment described in this chapter would take the equivalent of no more than 2 or 3 hours' wages.

As you read through this chapter, you will need to be discriminating as to which of these test instruments are worthwhile for you. That decision will primarily be based on the frequency of their use and the cost of downtime in *your* application.

Finally, you should be aware that the following sections describe only a small portion of the test equipment currently available. Even more so, the troubleshooting techniques in this chapter are a mere sampling of what you can do in the field to expedite your troubleshooting speed. If there is one lesson which I hope you will learn from this chapter, however, it is the value of improvising. If you can learn to devise appropriate testing techniques in your situation with the test equipment you have, the purpose of this chapter will have been achieved.

Brand-name equipment is specifically identified in this chapter. I have personally tested these instruments and can verify their effectiveness for the test conditions in which they are described. I do not intend, however, to suggest that only the instruments I have named are suitable for the testing conditions described. As you shop for test equipment, you will find many other makes of instruments which will serve you well for your troubleshooting work. The information in this chapter is merely intended as a guideline for your instrument selection.

Troubleshooting with Ammeters

The presence of a voltage on the terminal of an electrical component (or device) is not positive proof that the component is functioning. If the component itself is open, the voltage test will be inconclusive. On the other hand, if the component is open, the current draw will be zero. Thus, a current test will give additional information which is unavailable with only a voltage test.

The advantage of knowing a current value

Take the current test a step further. If the current draw is abnormal, something is faulty in the electrical component or device (or components if there are others in parallel). I will explain an "abnormal" current draw later, but for now (having added the current measurement), you now have three test values which can be used in your on-line troubleshooting work:

1. *The presence (or absence) of a voltage* at the electrical component (or device) terminal. (This is a test of the circuit up to the component, but tells you nothing about the condition of the component itself.)

2. *The presence (or absence) of a current draw* on the electrical component circuit.[1] (This test indicates that the component is electrically conductive, though it does not necessarily indicate whether or not it is operating normally.)

3. A *specific current value* which can be used as a comparison with the current draw of other similar electrical circuits. (This test compares the current value of the component under test with that of a similar component. In many cases, this test will establish whether or not the component is functioning normally.)

Let's try to illustrate what has been said in the three points above. Say you are troubleshooting a live circuit line on the ladder diagram used elsewhere in the book. The circuit you are testing has a relay at the end of the line. (Consequently, you are measuring the voltage and current draw of the relay coil.)

1. Your first test is a voltage test between the common grounded conductor and the wire to the relay coil. The multimeter reading is 120 V; therefore you know the circuit to the relay coil itself is complete.

2. Your second test is done with the your clamp-on ammeter set on the 10-A range. You get a reading of 0.29 A. You know that the coil is carrying a current, which means that it is not open. That is, the coil is operational.

---

[1] The voltage test, as it is being described here, must be done at the component's (or device's) terminal. The current test, however, can be done at any point along the circuit, since all parts of the circuit carry the full current value—assuming, of course, that there are no parallel legs on the circuit. This can be used to your advantage, since a full circuit check can be done at any point on the circuit. For instance, the presence of a current on a single limit switch wire would indicate that the circuit was—with some qualification—operational.

3. Your third test is on a similar relay coil circuit. It is only important that the second circuit which you are using for comparison is controlling a single relay identical to the actual circuit you are troubleshooting. In this case, the test result is 0.17 A. The reasons will be given later, but from this information you know that the relay drawing 0.29 A is not properly closing. Though the coil is operational, something is wrong with the mechanical part of the relay.

Though the above problem—a relay with a functional coil which is not mechanically closing—is an infrequent type of failure, you will occasionally encounter it. In this case, were you to shut down the system and examine the relay, you may find, for example, that the shading coil had broken, preventing the armature from seating. This could, of course, cause the relay contacts to remain open or seat poorly enough to cause premature burning and subsequent failure.

Evaluating the procedure

In this testing sequence you determined that the relay had a voltage across it which meant that it was drawing current. Normally, that would indicate an operative circuit. In this case, however, you were able to establish with additional ammeter values that the relay was not closing. By comparing the current draw of a similar relay with the one under test, you determined that the relay which proved to be defective was drawing too high a current.

A solenoid or relay (which are both electromechanical devices) will draw excessively high currents if the path for the magnetic flux is broken by separating the steel. If the armature (the moving steel part of the device) cannot move to its fully closed position, there will be an air gap, and the coil current will significantly increase. The amount of increase in specific amperage values is not the concern. Merely by comparing the component with a similar component in the circuit, it is possible to determine that the current draw is excessive.[2] From that, you have a basis for suspecting a mechanical (not an electrical) problem.

In Chapter 8 you learned how to read resistance to verify two parallel components in a single circuit. (The combined resistance of two identical electrical components is one-half the value of either of the components measured individually.) A clamp-on ammeter capable of

---

[2] Interestingly, a broken or displaced shading coil will not cause an increase in current, as long as the armature properly seats. The armature will be noisy, but the current will not be affected since the magnetic saturation of the steel has not changed with the loss of the shading coil winding. Only the phase displacement of the shaded area has changed; but a displacement change will not cause a measurable increase in the current draw.

reading low current values can perform the same function if the circuit is energized. In this case, however, the current values are added. That is, two parallel relays—each drawing 0.17 A—would draw 0.34 A on a single wire feeding both relays. Thus, you could test a parallel circuit in a similar manner. You would first take a current reading on a single component which was identical to the components on the parallel circuit you would subsequently be testing. In the final test on the parallel circuit, if the current value were double the value of the comparison circuit, you would know that both components were functioning. If, however, the value is equal to the comparison circuit, you would know that one of the parallel components is open.

Ammeter reading ranges

Before I give you an illustration of an ammeter used in testing a hydraulic solenoid circuit, I need to give you some specific information concerning clamp-on ammeters. Did you notice the current value assigned to the relay coil in the previous illustration? It was 0.17 A. In fact, this is the approximate current draw of an actual NEMA size 1 relay operating at 120 V AC. If you look at a standard ammeter, you will realize that this is well below the reading range of most clamp-on meters. (In all practicality, moving-coil meters could not be used for this type of testing.)

The Hioki digital clamp-on Hi Tester 3261 is capable, however, of this degree of precision. This instrument opens the door to some very sophisticated electrical troubleshooting. As mentioned at the beginning of Chapter 5, the Hioki digital clamp-on meter will read to two decimal points. (That is, it will read 0.00 A.) There are other meters such as the TIF 1000 series clamp-on ammeters which will read to one significant digit. (That is, the display will read 0.0 A. In the previous illustration, the 0.17 A reading would have been displayed as 0.2 A.) These meters can also be used for the testing described in this section. (Refer to Figure 9.1 for an example of both of these meters.)

Because of the extreme sensitivity of these ammeters when they are operating in the low ranges, there is a necessary precaution you must take to avoid inaccurate readings. The stray magnetic fields close to induction devices (relay coils or transformers) in the electrical panel can generate a reading on the meter. You will find that meter position becomes a variable. With no wire in the meter jaws, if you hold the jaws directly in front of the coil, you may read 0 A. By moving the meter to either side of the coil, the amperage reading will increase. (You obtain the zero reading when the jaws are in a position where the AC circuit is balanced. It is much like the zero reading you obtain when you clamp the ammeter jaws around both wires of an AC cir-

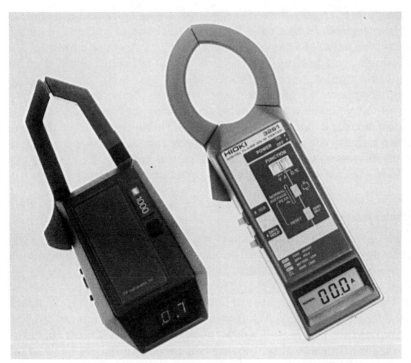

Figure 9.1 Two clamp-on ammeters which read low amperage values. The TIF 1000 can read 0.1 A (*left*) and the Hioki 3261 can read 0.01 A (*right*). (*TIF Instruments, Inc., and Hioki-RCC, Inc.*)

cuit.) Before putting the wire through the jaw of the ammeter for the actual test, it is necessary to hold the meter in the exact position of the test to determine if there is a value on the meter readout from stray magnetic fields. The most accurate testing is done by keeping the meter as far as possible from magnetic fields.

Actual ammeter testing

You are familiar with the mold-close circuit used in Chapter 5. (You can refer to Figure 5.5, or to line 22 in Appendix A for the circuit diagram—discount the jumper to line 23.) The final wire in the circuit is wire 15, which is connected to the mold-close solenoid (solenoid A). In the illustration you are about to study, you have a similar problem to the one you tested in Chapter 5; the mold will not close. You will test line 22 for a control voltage. In the first test, however, you will find that there is a control voltage to the solenoid itself. Thus, your testing will be confined to the solenoid to determine the fault. The machine is stalled on the nonfunctioning mold-close cycle.

Voltage verification test. Your first test will verify the voltage to the solenoid coil. You may use a voltmeter or a noncontact tester to verify the presence of the voltage. The test indicates a full control voltage on the solenoid lead wire 15. (*Note:* The presence of a voltage at the solenoid terminal does not indicate that the solenoid coil is functional. The coil could be faulty—though for the sake of this illustration, it is not.)

Current test

Test purpose. To verify that the solenoid coil is operational.

Test location. This test can be conducted on any wire in the circuit controlling solenoid A.

Test result. The ammeter indicates that the coil is drawing 1.4 A. You know that the circuit is complete and that the solenoid coil is operational.

Current comparison test

Test purpose. To verify the current draw of any other similar solenoid coil. (*Note:* Most solenoid coils will have an identification plate which lists the voltage and amperage of the coil. If that information is readily available, this second test may be unnecessary. However, you should also be able to see that it is often simpler to do this comparison test from the panel than it is to locate a hydraulic solenoid on the machine.)

Test location. This test will be conducted on a wire in any other energized circuit controlling a similar solenoid. [After studying the diagram in Appendix A, you have discovered that either low pressure close (solenoid W) or fast mold close (solenoid O) can operate simultaneously with the solenoid you are testing.] Your comparison test is taken on either solenoid W or solenoid O after setting the appropriate panel switches (SW8 and SW9).

Test result. The ammeter indicates that the solenoid coil chosen is drawing 0.8 A. Because this current draw is less than the current draw from the previous test (which was 1.4 A) you know that solenoid A (mold close) is electrically operational, but is mechanically faulty.

You learned earlier that when a relay armature fails to completely close (that is, when there is an air gap in the armature), the current draw will be excessively high. The same is true of a solenoid valve. In the testing example which was just given, you saw a solenoid valve which was rated at 0.8 A drawing 1.4 A. You could conclude from this that there was a mechanical problem in the valve which was preventing it from shifting. Whatever the mechanical problem would eventually prove to be, it is safe to go directly to the valve with no more electrical testing.

Let me anticipate a question: "Can I give a formula of current draw which will indicate the degree of the problem?" The answer is "no." This type of testing is merely done to compare a known normal value with an unknown value. Nonetheless, even though values cannot be assigned for the current, the testing procedure is extremely reliable and can save you a great deal of time in locating mechanical problems from the electrical panel.

Now, for the sake of interest, let me give you some values which I obtained from bench-testing an actual hydraulic solenoid valve. I was using a coil which was rated at 0.64 A. The total spool travel of the valve was 0.125 in. Using a clamp-on ammeter with two significant digits (0.00 A) I could read a tenth of an amp variation by moving the valve spool 0.002 to 0.003 in off its seat (that is, from the fully closed position). Moving the valve spool 0.020 in off its seat resulted in a current increase of 20 percent. At 0.050 in off its seat, there was a full 100 percent current increase.

The actual measurements and percentages are not significant in this illustration. What is significant is that the meter can detect such a small initial variation. A mechanically jammed spool valve would well be in the range where you would expect to find a very high current deviation from normal. (However, you would not find a deviation if the spool or armature were jammed in the fully closed position.) Do not try to take this information as the basis for test formulas. However, if you find a current variation between identical solenoid (or relay) coils of more than 10 or 15 percent, it merits further verification of the mechanical condition of the component.

Other ammeter tests

Other on-line troubleshooting can be done when you have the capability of measuring these very small current values.[3] Complete circuits

---

[3] You can increase the sensitivity of any ammeter by wrapping the conductor around the jaws. For example, if you wrapped the conductor around the jaws twice, you would multiply the actual value by 2, which gives a higher reading on the scale. If you made a jumper lead which was wrapped around the ammeter's jaws ten times, you would increase the reading by 10. (The jumper is used in series with the component you are testing.) With ten turns an 0.8-A measurement could be taken on a 15-A scale since it would read as 8 A. In this way, analog (moving-coil) meters can be used for lower-range measurements.

can be verified as operational by taking an ammeter reading at any point on that circuit. In other words, you could reduce your entire testing sequence to one test point in order to verify an entire ladder diagram circuit line *if the circuit is properly functioning.* By clamping the jaws of the meter around a limit switch wire you could verify that the entire circuit was operational. (If there is no current reading, however, you have no indication of where the break is and will need to rely on other troubleshooting techniques.)

The greatest difficulty with this testing procedure is the physical size of the ammeter jaws. It is often difficult to clamp the wire you want to test in the limited space available. Nonetheless, the concept of this testing procedure may well open very simple testing methods to your specific applications.

Some of the better-quality digital clamp-on meters have a "peak" hold function. (It is available on both the Hioki Hi Tester 3261 and TIF Instrument's TIF 1000.) There are a number of test procedures which can be done with this function. It is useful in determining motor starting current. Starting current values can often provide useful troubleshooting information when there are mechanical or electrical overload conditions. In normal motor start or run conditions, peak current values can be used to size fuses to maximum operating conditions. The peak can also be used as a comparison with normal currents if you are trying to locate a random surge. (The clamp-on meter can be left hanging on the conductor under test in the peak setting. If the equipment goes down because of a high current draw, the meter will record and hold the information until it is reset. For example, suppose you take a reading on a 20-A circuit and find that it is normally operating at 16 A, even though the circuit breaker is occasionally tripping. After hanging an ammeter on the conductor, you find a 24-A "peak" reading on the meter when the circuit breaker trips. You now know that some form of intermittent overcurrent condition exists which must be corrected.)

Troubleshooting Insulation Problems

Electrical malfunctions usually represent one of three broad categories: (1) the mechanical failure of a component (for example, the failure of the internal mechanism of a limit switch), (2) deterioration of electrical contact elements (for example, the excessive pitting and burning of relay contacts), and finally, (3) insulation failure (for example, internal grounding of motor windings). The majority of the troubleshooting procedures described in the early chapters of this book deal with component failures of some sort which are attributable to mechanical failures or deterioration of electrical contact elements.

The third cause of electrical malfunctions is that of insulation failure. Insulation failure, and insulation testing, is the subject of this section.

Electric motors

Electric motors are probably the most important—and certainly among the most frequently used—end users of electrical power in most industrial settings. Therefore, motor testing procedures are important in the overall troubleshooting program of any industrial plant.

I'm not going to discuss motor theory or construction in this chapter; it is a fascinating subject but it is outside of the scope of this book. However, the motor's insulation is another story. A motor which has failed will most frequently have an insulation-related problem. (Whatever condition outside of the motor initially caused the problem, the resultant motor winding heat will destroy the insulation, which is the immediate cause of motor burnout.)

A motor which has completely failed is generally easy to locate with a standard ohmmeter. If the insulation is charred, an ohmmeter reading to ground will show very low or zero resistance. A reading between leads may also indicate that they are open by indicating infinity [∞]. (When the motor has completely failed, your nose is as effective as any meter in your tool box. You just use the meter to sound "scientific" when explaining a $300 motor replacement. Can you imagine explaining to the accounting department that "My nose tells me that the pump motor should be replaced"?)

Since the subject of this book is fast troubleshooting, let's look at a simple procedure which can be used when verifying a totally damaged motor. (This motor will be completely shorted to ground. A motor that is in the early stages of insulation failure will require testing with a megohmmeter, which I will discuss later.) Rather than going to the motor itself and disconnecting wire nuts or terminal screws, it is much faster to open the motor controller (making certain that the power is off) and test from phase-to-phase and phase-to-ground with an ohmmeter on the motor side of the controller. This can result in significant time savings when the motor is buried deep in the machinery. If the test indicates very low resistance to ground or open windings, then your time is well spent in starting to work on the motor itself. If, on the other hand, the tests do not indicate abnormal conditions, you may want to look elsewhere before going to the effort of opening motor coverplates or disassembling the motor for a visual check.

The point I am making is this: You can check the condition of a motor just as accurately with an ohmmeter lead on the motor's supply line (at the motor's starter) as you can with the ohmmeter lead on the motor's wire terminal (inside the motor's electrical coverplate). Until you need to visually examine the interior of the motor, you have gained little by going to the effort of removing coverplates from the motor's terminal box. If the motor is open and accessible—and the motor controller is located 2 ft away—there may be little difference in which test point you choose. On the other hand, if the motor is inaccessible, then you will save a great deal of time by doing the testing from the most accessible point in the system. That obviously will be from a motor controller, or at times, in the electrical panel itself. Get into the habit of trusting your meter (within its limitations) rather than insisting on visual inspections which may have little effect on the accuracy of the actual test.

Insulation materials and failure

Before finishing this section with a description of megohmmeters and their use, let's take a quick look at insulation materials. Understanding what they are will help you understand what is happening when they fail.

Modern electric motors are wound with "magnet wire." Magnet wire includes a broad range of round and rectangular conductors used in coil windings for motors and transformers. Magnet wire has an enamel insulation coating. In fact, the term "enamel" may refer to any one of approximately 30 different insulation materials. Each of these materials has some advantage, whether it is in lower cost, higher temperature range stability, greater flexibility for handling during winding, or any of a number of other specialized characteristics. A chart of enamels includes such material names as acrylic, nylon, polyvinyl formal, epoxy, polyesters, and even ceramic materials. General-purpose enamels operate up to 105°C (or 221°F). Special-purpose enamels extend the range to higher limits.

There are other insulating materials besides the wire enamels used in general-purpose motor and transformer windings. After the windings are in place in the motor frame, they are often coated with baking varnishes or potted in epoxies. Oil-impregnated papers, fiber materials, and various plastics and rubbers are used as separating materials between coil groups or lead conductors.

What causes a motor to burn out? With the exception of grossly excessive current loads which actually cause the conductors to melt, almost all motor losses are a result of some form of insulation failure. Whether it is a progressive insulation deterioration over a period of years or rapid deterioration because of moisture or high current loads, the motor finally burned out because the insulation could no longer isolate the voltage differences in adjacent wires or coils.

Without trying to be highly technical, the reasons behind insulation failure can be classified into three broad categories:

1. *Heat-related breakdown.* This can be a long-term condition where organic materials in the insulation material degenerate to a point at which they can no longer provide the insulation values necessary for the application. It can also be caused by short-term conditions in which the insulation breaks down rapidly—a motor operating at 15 or 20 percent overload conditions with oversized thermal protection will quickly exceed acceptable temperature ranges, and may burn out in a matter of hours—or even minutes—of operation.

2. *Moisture-related breakdown.* Moisture is a major cause of insulation failure. Small droplets of water from condensation on the motor windings will cause arcing between conductors when the motor is restarted. At the point of the arcing, the organic materials will be carbonized as they are burned. This, in turn, becomes a conductive bridge between the conductors which will cause further arcing and heat.[4]

3. *Mechanical-related breakdown.* Insulation can be destroyed by mechanical problems such as vibration or physical contact with moving parts. I once replaced a pump motor which had burned out because a worn bearing allowed the rotor to touch the stator. The frictional heat caused a hot spot on the stator which resulted in a localized winding burnout.

Megohmmeter insulation testing

In each of the three causes of insulation failure given above, there will usually be early warning signs. The test instrument used to measure the insulation value of a winding is called a megohmmeter. Its name comes from its meg- (million) ohm resistance reading range. This instrument is used to test the resistance value of a winding under a load

---

[4] Properly installed motors which are subject to repeated contact with moisture will use a coil heater to keep the motor warm when it is shut down. If a motor's insulation is damp—but otherwise unharmed—it can be dried in one of several ways. External heat sources, such as heat lamps, can be directed on the coils. (However, excessive heat must be avoided.) A voltage of 5 to 7½ percent of nominal working voltage can be imposed on the stationary motor's windings as either long-term condensation prevention or as a means of drying the coils. A motor may also be run at no load with one-half (or less) nominal voltage until the windings are dry. (Be certain that the motor will start quickly, either on its own or with help.)

condition. (The value read on the megohmmeter scale is the insulation breakdown point given in ohms of resistance. The scale is in megohms. Therefore a reading of 500 on the scale means that at the test voltage produced by the meter, the insulation offers 500 million ohms of resistance.) The megohmmeter is called a "megger" in the trades.

An AC motor with good (and dry) insulation should read around 500 MΩ from phase to ground. If the motor has been in operation, it can be assumed that it is dry and should read this value plus or minus a small percentage. If the motor has been sitting where condensation has moistened the windings, the reading may be lower until the motor is dried. On the other hand, if the motor has been in operation and a reading of 300 MΩ or less is obtained, there is strong indication that the insulation is failing.

There are two types of megohmmeters—battery powered and magneto powered (refer to Figure 9.2). In both cases, a voltage is imposed on the windings being tested. The megohmmeter leads are used to energize the motor coil with high-voltage, low-current power. The simplest megohmmeters to use are battery-powered. These meters come in either 500- or 1000-V output models. (The higher-voltage models are generally the most expensive.) Megohmmeters use two leads and are operated and read much like a standard VOM multimeter. Magneto megohmmeters (which have a hand-crank magneto) are more cumbersome to use, though they produce a steady 1000-V output. They are capable of testing for high insulation values because of the high volt-

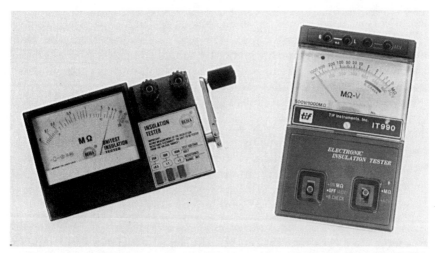

Figure 9.2 Two types of megohmmeters used for testing insulation: the Greenlee BEHA magneto-operated model 5778 (*left*) and the TIF IT990 battery-operated megohmmeter (*right*). (*Greenlee BEHA Corporation, and TIF Instruments, Inc.*)

age output which is independent of battery strength. (An example of the magneto type is Greenlee BEHA's insulation tester 5778. This is a high-quality megohmmeter which has three measuring ranges: 0 to 25 megΩ, 0 to 50 megΩ, and 0 to 100 megΩ. The output test voltages for these ranges are 250, 500, and 1000 V, respectively.)

There is a necessary caution when using a megohmmeter. Because the meter actually has an output of 500 or 1000 V, it must be used carefully. (I have never touched a "hot" megohmmeter lead. I am content to follow the manufacturers' directions when they say, "Don't do it!") Modern megohmmeters are nondestructive, which means they do not damage the motor windings during the test. However, there are certain kinds of tests for which the meter must never be used. Though you may test the windings of a single-phase motor, you must never have a capacitor (for a capacitor-start or capacitor-run motor) in the circuit while you are testing. The high voltage will puncture the capacitor. The same is true for solid-state equipment. Never use the megohmmeter on any solid-state circuits.

With this background in insulation and the function of a megommeter, you should be able to see its potential. You could use it much like the resistance tests I described earlier in this section. Now, however, by using the megohmmeter, you can do an actual resistance value test from the motor controller or motor disconnect. Let me show you how that can be done.

A refrigeration unit in our plant developed a leak which required a service call. Before the leak was discovered, there was indication that the compressor had been running hot. A week or two after the leak was repaired, the compressor blew a fuse and was shut down. It was obvious that it was time for some serious testing. This particular refrigeration unit has two circulation pumps powered from the main electrical circuit and one hermetically sealed compressor on a thermostatically controlled circuit with a starting relay. It is a three-phase, 240-V unit. The following tests were done:

1. A standard ohmmeter was used for the first testing. All three legs of the three-phase power-to-ground circuit tested as open. (That is, there were no indications of direct-ground shorts.) Secondly, both the circulation pump circuit and the compressor circuit were tested. The phase-to-phase circuits showed continuity across each set of motor windings and tested open across phase-to-ground.

2. A second group of phase-to-ground tests was done with a megommeter from the same test points. (I used a TIF IT990 Electronic Insulation Tester. This is a battery-operated tester. Though it lacks the 1000-V test capability, it is an excellent meter. It is a convenient megohmmeter to use for troubleshooting work.) In the second

test, I obtained a reading of approximately 500 MΩ from phase to ground on the circulating pump circuit. On the other hand, I obtained a reading of about 300 MΩ across the compressor terminals to ground. Since this last reading was less than the acceptable limit, there was strong evidence that the compressor was failing.

3. In order to verify my conclusion, I replaced the fuses and opened the compressor control switch. With just the circulation pumps on the circuit, the system operated normally with a current draw (measured with a clamp-on ammeter) within the expected operating range. I then turned on the compressor and immediately blew another fuse. Since the previous tests had shown that there was no ground fault, I knew the compressor was drawing excessive current—evidence that the compressor winding insulation was, in fact, failing. (I had also clamped a Hioki Hi Tester 3261 digital ammeter to the circuit. The ammeter reading was set on the peak current draw function, giving me the current value when the fuse failed. Again, the test results confirmed an internally shorted compressor motor.)

What I have not yet told you is how the testing was done. Since the two circulation pumps were in parallel with the main power supply, I only needed to find one test point for both pumps. However, since the main power supply came to the compressor starter relay, I was able to do all of the testing from a single point. The first test was from ground to each of the three-phase legs on the line side of the compressor relay. This single test provided a megohm test on the two pump motors, since they were in parallel. Finally, a test from ground to each of the three-phase legs on the compressor side of the starter relay provided a megohm test on the compressor. No wires were disconnected for the entire test.

The purpose behind this explanation is an illustration of troubleshooting speed. By carefully choosing my test points and by using an appropriate piece of test equipment, I was able to quickly and accurately locate the cause of the problem. There was no need to go directly to the motor terminals for the test. (Of course a verification of the test was done with the motor leads disconnected.) A megohmmeter is an excellent test meter for hermetic compressors because it is impossible to visually assess any part of the motor. For the same reason, however, it becomes an excellent time-saving troubleshooting meter for any motor. Why visually check the motor by removing coverplates when it can be done more quickly from the magnetic starter?

Troubleshooting Capacitor Problems

In Chapter 8 you were shown how to use a VOM to test capacitors for internal shorts. Proper capacitor testing, however, can be more complex than finding a simple short (though internal shorts are frequent faults which produce a completely worthless capacitor). Before a capacitor shorts, it will usually start to leak internally. There are specialized capacitor testers which will indicate that condition. (Refer to Figure 9.3 for an illustration of two typical capacitor testers.)

Capacitor use

Before talking about capacitor testing, let's take a short detour and look at the capacitor itself. Generally, you will find three uses of capacitors in industrial applications:

1. They are extensively used as starting capacitors on single-phase motors. Since single-phase motors in industrial plants are primarily fractional (less than 1 hp), capacitor use will be confined to small pumps, blowers, and the like.

2. A second use of capacitors is for power factor correction. (Power factor is the ratio of the actual power of an AC circuit to the apparent

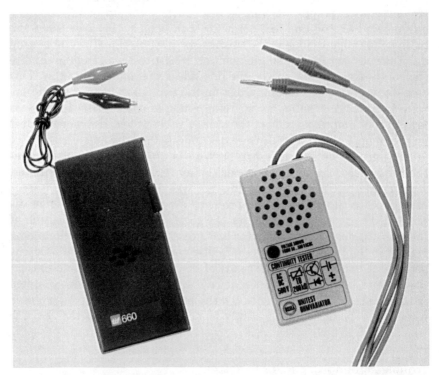

Figure 9.3 Two inexpensive capacitor testers: the TIF 660 (*left*) and the Greenlee BEHA 57002 (*right*). Both of these instruments will test for continuity. The Greenlee BEHA tester has additional functions. (*TIF Instruments, Inc., and Greenlee BEHA Corporation.*)

power as measured with an ammeter. Inductive loads from motors distort the power factor balance; the balance can be corrected with capacitance.) Capacitance produces a leading power factor and is often used to correct lagging power factor where large inductive (motor) loads are encountered.

3. Capacitors are used in DC applications. There will be power-conditioning capacitors in any circuit rectifying AC to DC.

Caution is always in order when working with capacitors since they can hold a voltage potential (a charge) even though the capacitor is disconnected. With even a small capacitor, the charge may be sufficient to damage a meter during testing. With large power-factor-correcting capacitors, the charge can be just as lethal as full line voltage. Always short the disconnected capacitor terminals with an insulated conductor before handling or testing.[5]

The established unit for capacitance is farads. [The farad is named in honor of the British scientist Michael Faraday (1791–1867).] Since, however, the farad is a large unit, general-use capacitors are rated in microfarads, which is one millionth of a farad. You will see this abbreviated as "mfd", "mf", or "μF".

Capacitor construction

A basic capacitor is constructed with two conductive (metal) plates separated by an insulator. The separator is called the dielectric. In use, positive electrons will accumulate on one plate while negative electrons accumulate on the other. The ability of the capacitor to hold a charge is based on two factors: the size in surface area of the plates and the thickness of the dielectric. (The thinner the dielectric, the greater the capacity. However, the breakdown limit of the capacitor is determined by the dielectric—or insulation—strength of the dielectric. Thus, dielectric material needs to be both thin and of a high insulation quality.) In actual construction, the plates are made of foil with a paper dielectric. This allows the capacitor to be rolled and sealed in a can.

The basic capacitor used in AC applications is a form called an electrolytic capacitor. An electrolytic capacitor is a modification which uses a single plate as one conductor and a chemical compound called an

---

[5] In Article 460, the National Electrical Code (NEC) requires that capacitors other than surge capacitors or capacitors included as a component part of other apparatus will have a means of draining the charge. It is specified that the voltage should drop to 50 V within one minute after being disconnected. But don't take chances. An old-style capacitor may not have the bleed resistor. Short out the capacitor terminals and be safe.

electrolyte for the other. The dielectric is a thin insulating film of oxide on the metal plate. Since the electrolytic capacitor is a DC device, the use of these capacitors for AC circuits requires an additional modification. An AC electrolytic capacitor has two plates (anodes) which are common to one electrolyte. Thus, in operation the two anodes are functioning alternately, which allows the capacitor to pass the AC current.

Capacitor failure

I have explained how capacitors are built because that is the simplest way to understand why they fail. A capacitor most often fails because the dielectric (insulation) is no longer doing its job. If the plates (whether plates alone or a plate and the electrolyte) touch each other, the capacitor will internally short and cannot hold a charge. There are generally two things which will cause a capacitor to fail:

Physical damage. If the capacitor can is crushed, or if the terminals are twisted or moved, the physical dislocation of the foil and dielectric may either reduce the dielectric strength or actually cause contact between the plates. Vibration in service is another leading cause of failure for the same reasons. In any of these cases, the capacitor becomes worthless.

Electrical damage. If the charge voltage on the opposing plates exceeds the insulation value of the dielectric, a spark will travel through the insulation to the other plate. The effect will be an actual hole in the insulation material. At the very least, this breakdown in the insulation will reduce the ability of the capacitor to hold a charge. This condition is identified as a "leaky" capacitor, which means it will not hold a full charge. The electrons will "leak" from one plate to the other. If conditions are severe enough, the spark may actually weld the two plates together. This condition is identified as a "shorted" capacitor. In the first case, a multimeter test might not indicate a problem since there is no actual continuity between the plates. The only totally accurate test is to load the capacitor to its working voltage and measure its ability to hold the charge.

There are two other conditions which you may encounter in capacitor testing. One is an "open" capacitor. For some reason (whether through physical abuse or electrical burning of the internal lead connections) the leads are not making contact with the plates. The other is a "grounded" capacitor. In this case, a lead or plate has come into electrical contact with the metal cover. Obviously, in either case, these capacitors are ready for the trash can.

Capacitor testing

You can set up a workbench test for a capacitor by measuring electrical values and the loss rates. However, this is not the kind of field testing which is either practical or fast. If you frequently work with capacitors, then specialized test equipment is in order. A number of manufacturers supply relatively inexpensive equipment for this purpose. TIF Instrument Company supplies a convenient hand-held capacitor tester TIF 660.[6] Two leads are connected to the disconnected (and discharged) capacitor terminals. An internal circuit loads the capacitor and indicates its condition by using a tone signal. The tone will indicate good, shorted, open, and leaking.

Troubleshooting an electrical circuit with capacitors will require some decisions on your part. Generally, with the exception of physical abuse or excessive voltage, capacitors are not the first candidates for testing. You may very successfully avoid testing individual capacitors and save time by that omission. On the other hand, if the capacitors have failed, they will adversely affect the circuit, and you may waste testing time until you come back to them for a satisfactory verification of their condition. In all cases where you are testing an individual capacitor, you need to isolate one of the capacitor's leads from the rest of the circuit, whether through an open switch or by disconnecting the lead itself. (If you have an oscilloscope, you don't need to disconnect leads. But if you have an oscilloscope, you are not in our league, anyway!)

Single-phase capacitor-start (or capacitor-run) motors which do not perform satisfactorily would require starting-winding testing which would include the capacitor. When a DC power supply in an electrical panel fails, the diodes are the first place to look. However, the capacitors may also need verification.

Troubleshooting with Phase Meters

A number of meters are available which indicate motor and phase rotation on three-phase wiring systems. (That is, these meters will indicate the direction of motor rotation after installation. They will also indicate the sequence of each of the three line phases.) Strictly speaking, their value is in installation work more than in troubleshooting.

---

[6] As is so often the case, this capacitor tester can be used for other noncapacitor test functions. The TIF 660 can equally be used as a continuity or diode tester.

Nonetheless, they are useful test instruments when the installation requirements merit them.

Reversing rotation of three-phase motors

One of the very practical advantages of three-phase motors is the ease of reversing their direction of rotation. A three-phase motor has three terminals. Reversing the connections of any two of these terminals will reverse the direction of the motor's rotation. (In other words, if a three-phase motor shaft is turning clockwise when terminal 1 is connected to phase A, terminal 2 is connected to phase B, and terminal 3 is connected to phase C, it will turn counterclockwise if terminal 1 is connected to phase B, terminal 2 is connected to phase A, and terminal 3 remains connected to phase C.)

It is obvious, however, that installing a three-phase motor requires careful attention to its wiring to avoid improper (and sometimes dangerous) motor reversal.

In many cases, a three-phase motor can be jogged (quickly started and stopped) to determine the direction of rotation before putting it into service. This presents no safety problems with an installation such as an air compressor since the motor can be briefly test run in either direction. If the direction of rotation is incorrect, the unit can be shut down while two leads are reversed. There are applications, however, in which a motor cannot be reversed without risking danger to either the equipment or personnel. Elevators, hoists, augers, door openers, and the like may need to be correctly wired before any testing is done. (If a hoist is wired in reverse, for example, the limit safety switches will not protect the system from overtravel. I once broke a chain on a 2-ton hoist learning that lesson the hard way!)

Using a phase-rotation indicator

There are two distinct test functions necessary for determining motor rotation. If you are installing a three-phase motor which must be assured of correct rotation before starting, you will need to perform both tests.

1. The first test is phase rotation, which means that you are testing the incoming lines for their phase sequence. (Properly generated three-phase power will sequence from phase AB, to phase BC, to phase CA.) Properly installed feeder lines will correspond with this sequence.

2. The second test is motor rotation, which means that you are testing the motor for its direction of rotation when it is connected to the presently installed lines.

Greenlee BEHA Corporation supplies a number of instruments which will perform these two tests. However, their model 5774 (Motor Rotation/Phase Sequence Indicator) combines both testing functions in a single meter. (Refer to Figure 9.4.)

Greenlee BEHA's meter is simple to use. For the first test, three color-coded test leads are connected to the incoming lines. (If you were installing or replacing a motor, these would be the lines L1, L2, and L3 in the magnetic starter.) Three neon lamps verify the condition of the lines. (If any one of the three lamps is not glowing, it indicates an open line.) A second set of neon lamps indicates normal- or reversed-phase rotation. (Normal-phase rotation would be lines L1, L2, and L3 sequencing from phase AB, to BC, to CA.)

The second test function is that of motor rotation. The three color-coded motor test leads are connected to the motor terminals T1, T2, and T3. (There is no line voltage applied to the motor during testing. The motor must be completely disconnected from any voltage source.) While the meter test button is depressed, the motor shaft is turned in the desired direction of rotation. (No more than a quarter turn is required.) A "correct rotation" or a "reverse rotation" lamp will glow, indicating the direction of rotation if the motor were wired according to the test leads.

For the actual motor installation, the motor terminals are wired to the corresponding lines according to the test results. (That is, the

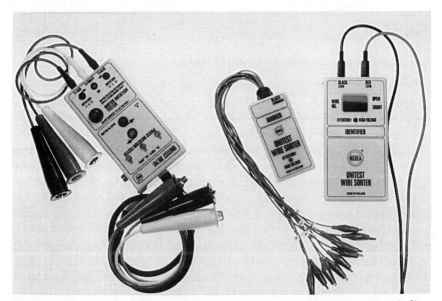

Figure 9.4 The Greenlee BEHA model 5774 motor rotation and phase sequence indicator (*left*), and the Greenlee BEHA model 5775 wire sorter (*right*). (*Greenlee BEHA Corporation.*)

known phase sequence of the incoming lines can be matched to the appropriate motor terminals when the motor test is correct. This will result in a known direction of motor rotation.)

Once an electrician is familiar with the operation of this meter, it should take less than a minute to test a motor hookup during installation. Assuming that the necessary safety precautions have been taken, the actual hot leads at the motor (coming from the magnetic starter) could be connected to the phase-rotation portion of the meter. With the motor disconnected, the color-coded motor test leads would be connected to the motor terminals. The two tests would be performed, comparing the direction of rotation for each. If both tests indicated the same direction of rotation, the motor terminals and line wires would be connected according to the meter's color-coded test leads. If the test indicated a dissimilar direction of rotation, two motor terminals would be reversed when the terminals were connected to the line. Of course, the lines are deenergized after the testing—no installation work is done with hot lines.

The value of this type of testing prior to motor installation will greatly depend on the type and frequency of work you are doing as an electrician. If you are working where startup testing is impossible or costly—or where reversed motors would be hazardous—the cost of phase-rotation meters is worthwhile.

In keeping with this book's objective of reducing machine downtime and increasing plant productivity, phase-rotation test equipment may offer substantial time savings in specialized situations.

Troubleshooting with Wire Identification Instruments

There are a number of wire-sorting instruments available from various suppliers. Most are similar in operation. An easy-to-use (and reasonably priced) model is Greenlee BEHA's Unitest Wire Sorter (see Figure 9.4). This instrument has two units; the "Marker" unit has ten numbered leads and a common conductor. The "Identifier" unit has one test lead and a common conductor. The Identifier uses a LED number display (from 0 to 9, which represents ten possibilities) for the wire identification. There are two additional LEDs; the first indicates that the circuit under test is open, the second indicates that the circuit under test is shorted (or has continuity with the common circuit). Both the Marker and the Identifier also have a LED line voltage warning indicator, inasmuch as the units cannot be used with any voltage on the line. Any number of wires from one to ten may be tested at a given time.

Using a wire-sorting instrument

Before using the Greenlee BEHA Wire Sorter, it is important to verify that the circuits being tested are deenergized. The common leads of both of the units are then grounded (or connected to a known common wire). The actual testing is carried out by clipping the numbered leads of the Marker to the unknown conductors in the circuit. When the other end of the circuit is touched with the Identifier probe, the correct lead number will be displayed in the readout window. If the test probe is held against a circuit which is common to none of the Marker's leads, the "open" LED will glow. If the test probe is held against a circuit that is shorted, the "short" LED will glow.

Who needs a wire sorter? In answer, let me tell you an electrical horror story. I once saw a production machine which had been "moved" by a butcher—the entire control panel had been separated from the machine by hacksawing the umbilical leads. To correct that stroke of genius, you would need a wire sorter! (If you were reconnecting the 200 plus wires—all the wires were conveniently color-coded "standard red"—you would undoubtedly start by identifying a set of wires from the panel to the cut using the wire sorter. This would give you correctly numbered wires at the cut on the panel side. Then you would open covers and identify wire numbers on the machine by reading the wire identification labels. Using the wire sorter, you would then identify the wire number on the machine side of the cut and splice as you finished each identified pair. Any method would take time, but the wire sorter would allow you to work in groups of ten wires rather than with single wires as you would be doing with a continuity tester.)

There are many less dramatic cases in which you might use a wire sorter. I have used it to verify wiring harnesses and thermocouple leads. (It could also be used to identify the positive and negative sides of thermocouple pairs.) In Chapter 10, I will be showing you how to identify unmarked wires with a long test lead and a meter. The wire sorter could make that job much simpler since you could identify a number of wires from a single hookup without the necessity of the long lead.

Similar to the procedure of the last paragraph, you could determine the operation (and wire identification) of multiple-function switches. If you were testing a limit switch, you might connect the number 1 lead of the Marker to the normally open side of the switch, and the number 2 lead to the normally closed side. You could verify that the switch was functioning correctly if the Identifier changed from lead 1 to lead 2 as the switch was cycled back and forth. (The Identifier clip would be placed on the common switch supply wire.) You could use the same procedure in more complex applications where you were verifying the operation of large numbers of conductors and switches. Of course, you would need to keep a notepad with number references since the ten numbers on the wire sorter (from 0 to 9) would have no bearing on the actual wire numbers of the machine.

Greenlee BEHA's Wire Sorter can be used as a short tester with the ability to identify the specific grounded circuit. If you were to clip a Marker lead to each of a group of questionable wires and successively touch the probe to each of them (you can touch the alligator clip of the Marker leads—there is no need to have any distance in the conductor) the Identifier will show a number for each of the ungrounded conductors and will indicate "short" for the grounded conductor(s).

The Greenlee BEHA Wire Sorter can also be used as a continuity tester. Only the Identifier unit is needed for this test and is used as a conventional continuity meter. When the two leads are touched to a common conductor, the "short" LED will light.

Be aware, however, that this type of instrument can only be used on deenergized circuits. Do not try to do on-line troubleshooting with this or any other type of specialized identification equipment.

Do you need a wire sorter? Needless to say, you can identify conductors just as accurately with a multimeter as you can with a wire sorter. However, you cannot do it nearly as quickly, and you will have more difficulty as the distance increases between your test points. Therefore, the question is really a matter of how frequently you would be using the wire sorter, and the total cost of the added downtime required for the slower procedure when using a multimeter. An added benefit with a wire sorter—as with any piece of specialized test equipment—is that you may discover other uses for it (such as the switch testing described above) which may justify its purchase price.

Troubleshooting with a Neon Lamp

I am going to have some fun with this last test instrument. After you have been tempted with expensive solid-state equipment that can literally analyze every fault in the electrical circuits you are testing, it's time to come back to the basics.

If you are on-line troubleshooting a faulty circuit, you are simply trying to find one thing—an "open" in the circuit. In Chapter 8 you were shown how to use a VOM or DVM to locate the problem.

If a VOM or DVM will give you your troubleshooting information by indicating the presence of a voltage, why can't you do the same thing with nothing more than a $3 neon glow lamp? (The glow lamp, as you know, is nothing but a resistor-protected neon lamp in a molded plastic case. It has two 6-in leads which are touched on the bare conductors. It will glow if it is across 60 V or more.)

I am not suggesting that all which has been said in praise of the new generation of meters is oversell. I would dread having nothing but a neon lamp—or even a VOM—for my troubleshooting work. At the same time, I want you to realize that, as important as good instruments are, the skill of the troubleshooting electrician is still the most valuable asset for effective diagnostic work.

Could you troubleshoot with only a neon test lamp? Yes![7] A knowledgeable electrician might do more with only the test lamp than a poorly prepared electrician could do with a box full of test instruments. (OK then, what could a knowledgeable electrician do with a box full of test instruments?)

Chapter Review

Troubleshooting speed can often be increased through a careful selection of specialized testing equipment in conjunction with a thoughtful and innovative approach to its use. Even though this chapter merely touched on some possible troubleshooting alternatives, their suggestion should supply a basis for the development of innovative testing techniques in your specific field of application.

A clamp-on ammeter can often be used to determine if the electrical component or device at the end of the circuit is functioning normally. The presence of a voltage to the component's terminals is often inconclusive, whereas a current draw—measured with an ammeter—can give a more accurate indication of the condition of the component. When the ammeter is capable of reading very small current values, its applications for troubleshooting electrical controls in a panel or on the machine are greatly enhanced. Examples of diagnostic troubleshooting were given where the current values of improperly functioning relays or solenoids were compared with normal values. Examples of specialized ammeter functions—such as "peak" value holding—were given with an explanation of their value in on-line troubleshooting work.

Insulation testing equipment—specifically megohmmeters—is useful for troubleshooting work. You were encouraged to take phase-to-ground readings from the most accessible site on the machinery. In most cases, this would be from the motor contactor or a fused discon-

---

[7] You could use a neon test lamp and exactly duplicate the first three troubleshooting steps as given in Chapter 8, Troubleshooting with the Multimeter.

nect. By taking your first readings from these readily accessible areas, a great deal of time can be saved by avoiding the unnecessary location of testing terminals on the motor itself. The visual and meter inspection of the actual motor should take place only after there is reasonable certainty that the motor is at fault.

A general discussion of the cause of motor burnout identified three major causes, all dealing with insulation failure. They are:

1. Heat-related insulation breakdown

2. Moisture-related insulation breakdown

3. Mechanical-related insulation breakdown

Insulation failure can be determined with the use of the megohmmeter. This testing can often be done from points outside the motor such as the motor contactor. Because of the high inherent test voltage output of the megohmmeter (500 to 1000 V), this test instrument must never be used on capacitors or solid-state circuits.

Capacitors are constructed with two conductive plates separated by an insulating dielectric. Capacitor failure is generally in the form of a breakdown in the dielectric or a short between the plates. Capacitors must be handled carefully—they can hold a charge which can be damaging to test equipment or potentially hazardous to personnel if the terminals are not shorted. Special capacitor testers are available which will indicate the various fault conditions of a capacitor.

Other specialized equipment is available which can be an asset in troubleshooting work. Phase-rotation meters can be used to identify leads and establish motor rotation. A wire identification meter can be used for various troubleshooting problems beyond mere wire numbering. This would include the identification of control wires in other parts of the circuit, identifying thermocouple leads and wire harness terminals, and similar types of identification work.

The chapter closed by taking you back to the simplest of testing tools—the neon lamp. The purpose was to remind you that the measure of the electrician is not in the quantity of specialized tools he or she carries. Rather, the true measure is in the electrician's ability to use knowledge—and then tools as necessary—to come to quick and effective troubleshooting solutions.

Chapter Questions

Thinking through the text

1. Why is the presence of a voltage on the wire leading to an electrical component (or device) inconclusive evidence that the component itself is functioning?

2. What three test values can you work with in on-line troubleshooting? What does each value indicate?

3. What type of meter would be used to indicate that a solenoid or relay was not moving to a fully closed position? How would the reading vary from a normal reading?

4. Irrespective of the initial outside condition which causes a motor problem, what is generally the immediate cause of motor burnout?

5. When testing a motor for insulation failure, two tests are conducted with an ohmmeter or a megohmmeter: phase-to-phase and phase-to-ground tests. What are the test points for these two tests? (That is, where are the meter's test leads placed to complete the tests?)

6. What are the three broad causes of insulation failure?

7. Two testing conditions are named in which a megohmmeter must never be used. What are they? What is the reason a megohmmeter cannot be used for these tests?

8. What are the three most frequent uses of capacitors in industrial settings? What caution is given before handling or testing capacitors?

9. What are the two primary causes of capacitor failure? Briefly explain each.

10. How do you reverse the direction of rotation of a three-phase motor?

11. What does the author identify as the most valuable asset for effective troubleshooting?

Deepening your electrical understanding

12. Voltage and current are distinctly different values. The significance of these values for on-line troubleshooting is dependent on the condition of the electrical component at the end of the control circuit. If the electrical component is fully operational, either a voltage or current test is indicative of a functioning circuit. On the other hand, if the component is electrically open, the voltage test may be normal, though the current test will register zero. Why is this true? How can you apply these two test results to reach a conclusion about the condition of an electrical component?

13. From your own troubleshooting experience, can you describe a situation where the capability of reading very small amperage values could be beneficial in either ease of verifying the circuit's operation or in increasing the speed of the troubleshooting process?

14. A megohmmeter reading of 300 MΩ to ground for an electric motor is low. What you do about it, however, may depend on other circumstances.

What might you conclude if this motor has regularly been in service and has tripped its thermal overloads? What might you conclude if this motor had been in storage in a damp area? In the latter case, how would you attempt to remedy the low insulation resistance reading?

15. If you are replacing a capacitor in a single-phase electric motor—but are unable to buy an exact replacement size—you can substitute a capacitor with an approximate capacity in microfarads, but you must use a capacitor with an equal or higher voltage value. From what you learned about the construction of capacitors (particularly as it relates to the dielectric), why is it important that you never substitute a capacitor with a lower working voltage value?

10

Expanding On-Line Troubleshooting Applications

In this chapter you will discover how to apply the basic on-line troubleshooting skills which you have learned to other types of electrical circuits and problems. Specifically, you will see how to make application to both more complex and simpler circuits. You will also be shown how to do your troubleshooting when you have no ladder diagram information.

Up to this point in the book, you have been working with line segments of a moderately sized ladder diagram. In fact, if you are currently servicing equipment in an industrial plant, you will see many electrical circuit diagrams which are similar to the one you are studying in this book; they will be similar in their complexity and types of circuits.

However, if you have grasped the significance of the troubleshooting information you have studied so far, you will realize that increased size and complexity in a ladder diagram is not a question of new kinds of information; rather, it is simply a matter of adding more of the same information you have already been dealing with. (In the case of a more simplified diagram, it will be a matter of reducing the number of circuits, not a matter of changing the type of presentation.)

If you understand the basic electrical symbols used on a diagram, its complexity (or simplicity) is merely a matter of dealing with more (or fewer) circuit functions. It is not a problem of dealing with new forms of information. You presently have all of the basic information necessary in order to successfully use any electrical diagram you might encounter.

Reading Complex Electrical Diagrams

Very possibly, you may need to troubleshoot a piece of equipment which has enough electrical drawings to wallpaper your kitchen. Your first reaction is to drop your meter and then claim you can't do any troubleshooting until it is replaced. However, if you carefully look at the drawings before panicking, you will realize that the drawing complexity does not come from the need to understand new symbols or drawing formats. The complexity is merely in the number of circuits you will be dealing with. If you logically work through the new material with the information you already know, you should have little increased difficulty in understanding the diagram.

You will still use your basic ladder diagram reading skills with a complex diagram. As in any ladder diagram, each circuit will be represented as a line running from left to right on the drawing. There are some differences, however, which you will expect to see:

1. *More circuit areas will be involved.* In all likelihood, the more complex the diagram, the more you will find widely displaced electrical functions represented on a single circuit line. A simple diagram may have two or three relay or switching points on a line which are physically close to each other in the actual electrical panel. As the electrical diagram grows, you will find functions on a single line which represent widely separated physical locations or switches and relays, as well as the involvement of numerous electrical circuits and functions. Consequently, you will need to be aware of many more parts of the circuit to do your basic checking. Nonetheless, the testing procedure is the same.

2. *Circuits will be symbolically divided.* As the circuit grows, it becomes increasingly difficult to keep related circuits close to each other on the drawing. For this reason, you will see a greater use of separated circuits. (Refer to Chapter 2 for a discussion of the symbols representing separated circuits.) Any circuit malfunction will demand more care on your part so that you do not overlook continuations of circuits in other areas of the diagram. That is particularly true of parallel circuits which have an influence on the circuit you are testing. There will also be a greater use of widely separated mechanically connected functions, such as double-throw limit switches and multifunction push buttons and switches.

3. *There may be a greater use of specialized symbols.* Though not always so, in many cases a more complex diagram will also include

more specialized symbols. Thus, you may have various thermal, pressure, or other specialized limit switches indicated on the diagram. In addition, there may be a greater use of solid-state equipment and their related symbols.

The basic guideline in working with complex diagrams is to isolate the test areas into small segments of the diagram. Once you have narrowed the area of the diagram (and the machine's functions) to a manageable area on the diagram, the testing procedures will be the same as those you have used with simpler diagrams.

Simple Wire Diagrams

You will often find wire diagrams in equipment with limited electrical circuits. This is particularly true of self-contained motor and motor overload circuits. For example, in Figure 3.3 you have a wire diagram for a refrigeration compressor motor circuit. This type of diagram is often attached inside the terminal cover. (You were given an explanation of wire diagrams, as opposed to ladder or line diagrams, in Chapter 3. As you remember, the wire diagram is a physical representation of the circuit. That is, components are located in relationship to each other as you would see them in the actual equipment, whereas in the ladder diagram they are represented schematically.)

Reading this diagram should not give you any difficulty. The actual symbols are essentially the same as those used in the ladder diagram. However, the wire diagram will arrange the drawing according to the physical layout of the electrical equipment it represents. (This is in contrast to the ladder diagram, which will lay all of the circuit components on a horizontal line irrespective of their actual physical location in the equipment.)

For the purpose of troubleshooting, you can use this diagram in the same way you have used the ladder diagram. If you are using on-line troubleshooting techniques, you would trace through the live circuit checking for an open conductor. If you have taken the equipment off-line, you would check for open conductors by doing resistance (or conventional continuity) measurements. In any case, the testing procedure will be much like you have done elsewhere in this text.

You may also find that more is left to your assumed knowledge with less complex equipment. For example, in the refrigeration unit from which Figure 3.3 comes, there may be no additional circuit information even though there may be a motor relay, refrigeration cut-out switches, fuses, and a control switch in the actual circuit. Because of its simplicity, however, the manufacturer may not supply a ladder diagram of the complete circuit. If you are troubleshooting the unit, you may also be required to do some basic testing (visual and otherwise) to determine the actual circuit. Again, this does not need to be difficult. With your ability to do various types of continuity tests (both on-line and dead circuit) you can quickly trace circuits by testing from a known starting point (say, for example, from a fuse terminal) to a final control point (for example, one side of the relay coil). If the part of the circuit you have just tested is functioning, you may need to continue testing in order to identify circuit functions.

Troubleshooting without Diagrams

Some day you will open a panel full of relays and wires and be asked to "fix it," but you will have no ladder diagram. That's never good news. However, with the information in this section, you can keep the lack of the ladder diagram from being a total disaster.

There is no single formula to use when troubleshooting without a diagram. Nonetheless, there are techniques you can use to greatly reduce the confusion. In this section, I will show you one way to get started. (From your own experience, you will find other workable procedures. Don't be afraid to experiment.) Since you are troubleshooting without a diagram, I will explain what is being done; you will need to use your imagination more because there are no specific references to wire and identification numbers.

Your initial testing sequence

Now your work begins. You have been called to a manufacturing plant to check a nonfunctioning ejector system on a plastic injection molding machine. The company has no ladder diagrams for this machine. The machine has been shut down, and they want you to get it back on-line. (To simplify the illustration, I will let you get through the preliminary steps of your investigation without recording it here.) Finally, however, you concur that the ejector system is truly at fault as you have been told. For simplicity's sake, as in the illustration of the ejector system in Chapter 8, you can verify the hydraulic solenoids with the manual ejection push button; fortunately, the present electrical problem is confined to the automatic functions. Your first step will be to isolate the electrical device (a solenoid in this case) which is not functioning. That will be the starting point for your subsequent testing.

Locating a nonfunctioning solenoid.   There are three ways in which you might locate the hydraulic solenoid which activates the ejection system. The first, and simplest, is to find the location from some information source other than the missing electrical drawings. The operator's handbook may list each of the solenoids and its function, there may be hydraulic diagrams available which will give the information, or the solenoids themselves may have a descriptive tag on them.

The second way to locate the solenoid is through its operation. In this case, since you can use the manual push button, you might have an assistant cycle the ejector while you look for the physical location of the solenoid. (You should be able to hear or feel the solenoid "click" when it is cycled.)

The final way to locate the solenoid is the most difficult and demands the most care for the sake of safety. In this case, you would trace the ejector cylinder's hydraulic lines back to a hydraulic valve or manifold block. This may identify the valve (and solenoid) or it may identify two or three possibilities. You can now verify the correct valve by manually pushing the actuating pin on the solenoid. (In almost every case, a hydraulic solenoid valve will have a push rod which is used to manually cycle the solenoid.) Thus, by watching the ejector system, you can verify the solenoid by its function. (Needless to say, this procedure takes special care, since it is done with the hydraulic pumps running. The machine must be set so that the actuation of the wrong solenoid will not damage the machine or injure personnel. You must also remember that you have bypassed all limit switches, stroke safeties, and electrical interlocks by manually activating the solenoid.) Be certain that you know what you are doing before attempting this test procedure.

Electrical testing from the known electrical device.   The purpose of your testing is to work back from the known, nonfunctioning electrical device to find the circuit problem (see Figure 10.1). You should be able to remove the solenoid cover and identify the wire number of the circuit feeding that solenoid. Testing from this wire number is the next step in your testing sequence.

What do you do if there are no wire identification numbers on the solenoid wires? You may want to have some Kentucky Fried Chicken sent in—this may take longer than planned! (The wire identification tags are often missing when wires have been reconnected a number of times.) However, if you kill the electrical circuit and do some careful continuity testing, you can find your wire number relatively easily. Disconnect both leads from the solenoid. Attach a test wire which is long enough to reach the electrical panel to one of the two wires under the solenoid cover which supply the solenoid. (Use only the supply wires, not the solenoid leads.) Make a first test to the grounded common. Change the test lead on the two wires feeding the solenoid until you find continuity. You can now identify that wire as the common. Unless the common wire itself is damaged it is of no value to you as a part of the test, so you should identify it (by reconnecting it to the so-

Figure 10.1 Using a wire identification instrument to locate solenoid control wires in the panel. This procedure may be used to identify circuits if wire labels are missing. (*Test Instrument from Greenlee BEHA Corporation.*)

lenoid coil) and begin your test with the hot wire. Connect your test lead to the remaining solenoid supply wire and again use your meter to find continuity with a numbered wire in the electrical panel. By touching each of the wires on the terminal block(s), you should find one which shows continuity. That is, of course, the wire—and the identification number—which is controlling the unidentified solenoid. If none of the terminal block numbers indicate continuity, you may need to test in other parts of the machine as described above.

Testing toward the fault. You now have a wire number which you know should be energized. You might wish to verify this by running the machine until it stalls and then taking a voltage reading on the wire number you have identified. The reading would be zero volts if you have identified the correct wire and if the solenoid coil is not the cause of the malfunction. You will now begin your testing from this wire number back to the hot side of the circuit.

Actual troubleshooting procedures

There would be times during the testing in which you could use on-line troubleshooting with a live circuit. However, when you are testing limit switches which are next to moving equipment, extreme caution must be exercised lest the machine cycle. Generally, if you are tracing a circuit through the actual machine, it is recommended that you completely deenergize the prime movers (motors). If you can locate the necessary wire numbers in the electrical panel, you might wish to stall the machine and use on-line procedures, provided that you can satisfy all necessary safety precautions.

Your present testing objective is to identify each end of the numbered wires in the ejector solenoid circuit. If, for example, you determine that the wire to the solenoid is wire 47, you need to find this same wire number on a relay or other switch. On the point at which this wire terminates, you have a switched point (a relay contact or a switch of some kind) which must be inspected. If wire 47 terminates a given relay, you must trace across the relay contacts to identify the next wire number. You will, of course, verify the condition of each switching point (relay contacts, limit switch, etc.) in the circuit as you progress. If wire 47 terminates on a relay contact that closes across wire 126, then your next step will be to locate the other end of wire 126, check that point for conductivity, and proceed to the next wire number. If, for instance, you find more than a single wire at any terminal, you know that you need to trace multiple termination points. If two wires are labeled as 47 on the first relay you found, you must trace both 47 wires to their sources and perform tests on each of those circuits. As you work, you will need to draw the developing diagram and keep notes.

This step-by-step testing will take you to many parts of the machine. A wire number may have only one termination point in the panel. (It may be obvious that the wire is routed from the panel terminal block to a line exiting the panel.) You will then need to trace that wire to a control point such as a switch panel or limit switch. At this point, you will need to open panel and switch covers to determine wire numbers and locations.[1] With the covers off, you can check that specific switch for continuity, moving the switch to check its operation in both its open and closed positions. (See Figure 10.2.)

When you are tracing wires outside of the electrical panel, you can use conduits and wire channels as location indicators. If you were try-

---

[1] However, you can often do some knowledgeable guessing at this point. Wire numbers across a single switch are often sequential. Thus, if wire 47 leaves the panel, and wire 48 returns to the panel, you might check across these wires to see if they are common. A circuit often has wire numbers which are close in numerical sequence.

Figure 10.2 Using a proximity (voltage) tester at an accessible midpoint in the circuit. If the tester indicates the presence of a voltage, you know the circuit is functional to this point. (*Greenlee BEHA Corporation.*)

ing to locate a termination point for an ejector-related circuit wire, you would first trace the wire in the panel to a specific conduit exiting the panel. That conduit would then go to a given part of the machine, either directly or via a wire channel. If any of the limit switches on the ejector system were fed by that conduit or wire channel, they would be the first switches to check for the given wire numbers.

As you locate and record the electrical diagram for the circuit you are testing, you should draw the diagram with the appropriate electrical symbols. Your troubleshooting techniques for the circuit components will be much the same as described in other sections of the book. The difference, however, would come only in the thoroughness of your testing as you move from section to section. Since it would take considerable time to draw the entire diagram, it is a better use of time to completely check each area of the circuit as you move through it (hoping that you will find the problem early). There is little value in drawing the diagram beyond the point of the system failure.

Expanding Your Troubleshooting Capabilities

The major objective of this book is to give you the basic techniques for quickly troubleshooting industrial equipment with the aid of electrical (ladder) diagrams. That has been achieved (I trust!) by teaching you how to read electrical diagrams, giving you an introduction to some of the test equipment which is currently available, and explaining a troubleshooting technique which can greatly increase your diagnostic speed.

If you have grasped the basic principles of troubleshooting which I have explained to this point, you have a good foundation for your own work in the field. It is impossible, in a book of this size, to cover every conceivable type of electrical testing. Furthermore, there are significant areas which have had little (or no) coverage at all in the book. Nonetheless, if you can use the techniques covered in this text, you will have little difficulty adapting your skills to the particular needs of your specific job requirements.

Distinguish yourself as a competent electrician who is fast—who is very fast!—in your troubleshooting skills. You will gain your employer's appreciation and you will increase your self-confidence as you develop professionally.

But there is more which we as electricians can achieve in our profession than merely installing and troubleshooting equipment.

In the last two chapters of this book I am going to take you away from electrical diagrams, beeping test instruments, and burned relay contacts. I want you to be a very good electrician and troubleshooter. Even though I trust you have made a good start in that direction through the first ten chapters, I know that there is much more to the subject than I could ever teach you. There is much more to the field of electrical work than troubleshooting. Therefore, in the last chapters, I want to broaden your horizons. If you can take it upon yourself to grow—and to become increasingly knowledgeable in the broad field of electrical work—you can stretch your potential far beyond your peers who are content to merely put in their day's work.

Make it your goal to become the best electrician possible!

Chapter Review

Once you understand the basic concepts represented in electrical symbols and ladder (or wire) diagrams, the complexity or simplicity of a particular diagram is inconsequential.

In diagrams of greater complexity (that is, diagrams with a larger number of circuits), you will be dealing with more widely displaced electrical functions represented in single circuit areas; you will find that the circuits are symbolically divided more throughout the drawing; and you may find a greater diversity of specialized symbols. Nonetheless, these differences should cause you little difficulty in the actual use of the diagram if you isolate the test areas into small segments of the diagram.

Equally, simple wire diagrams should cause you no difficulty since they will also use basic electrical symbols. The wire diagram will represent the physical layout of the circuit rather than the schematic layout of the ladder (or line) diagram. When troubleshooting simple circuits or using simple wire diagrams, you may need to verify undesignated areas of the circuit through actual testing.

Troubleshooting without the aid of a diagram was also explained. Though you will need to develop applicable techniques for each situation, the suggestion in this chapter was to identify the known—but nonfunctioning—electrical device as the first step. Then, by identifying each wire number in reverse order, you can test backward toward the circuit fault. Specific suggestions were given for determining the wire numbers and the control contacts and switches in the circuit. Though on-line troubleshooting techniques may be used at certain times in this testing procedure, special cautions were given with the recommendation that far greater use of dead circuit testing be used. If the testing becomes extensive, you will need to draw the diagram as you work in order to properly identify and locate circuit areas for further testing.

In the closing paragraphs of the chapter, it was suggested that the truly professional electrician is one who is concerned, not only with the quality of his or her troubleshooting work, but equally with increasing personal electrical and related knowledge.

Chapter Questions

Thinking through the text

1. In comparing the diagrams you have studied in previous chapters with more complex diagrams, what information change would you expect to see in the complex diagram?

2. Briefly list and explain the three differences you might see in a more complex diagram.

3. What basic guideline is given for working with complex circuits which will result in testing procedures similar to those with which you are already familiar?

4. What is the lay-out difference between a wire diagram and a ladder (or line) diagram?

5. List the three ways in which a hydraulic solenoid valve for a known function may be located. What are the specific safety concerns for the third method?

6. After identifying the numbered wire connected to the final electrical device, what is the objective of each testing sequence?

7. When tracing a wire outside of the electrical panel, what might help you in determining the locations of switches in other parts of the machine?

Deepening your electrical understanding

8. In what way do circuits which have a larger number of symbolic divisions (that is, separated circuits) demand more care during troubleshooting? Why is there a special caution with parallel circuits?

9. When you are working without an electrical diagram, your testing will most likely start from the known electrical device which is not functioning. In your opinion, what advantages does this have as the preferred starting point? You were also told that there is no single prescribed way to troubleshoot when you must work without a diagram. Can you suggest conditions under which you might start at a different location?

10. A procedure for identifying a wire number is described wherein a long test lead is attached to an unnumbered wire and subsequently used for a continuity test which will identify the wire number. Can you suggest other uses for this long-lead continuity (resistance) test?

11. Why do you think there are greater safety concerns with the testing described in this chapter than there might be in the standard on-line troubleshooting procedures when using a ladder diagram? Under what conditions might you occasionally be able to safely use on-line troubleshooting while testing as described in this chapter?

Broadening the
Electrician's Horizons

In this chapter, you, as a maintenance electrician,
will be encouraged to broaden your knowledge
beyond mere electrical skills. You will then be
given specific techniques for increasing your
general knowledge in all areas of your work.

The Place for Broader Knowledge

Helping you become more effective in your electrical troubleshooting is the underlying purpose of this book. You will achieve effectiveness in many ways. In the early chapters of this book, the information regarding diagram reading, troubleshooting procedures, and the availability of test instruments was oriented toward increasing your effectiveness as an electrician.

The techniques and skills of electrical work are important. However, unless they are balanced with in-depth understanding and knowledge, you will fail to achieve your full potential as an electrician.

Defining effective electrical work

Effectiveness is relatively easy to determine. It is based on the interrelationship of the speed of the troubleshooting process (measured as the total machinery downtime), the reliability of the diagnosis and repair (measured by the absence of future downtime caused by undiagnosed or poorly repaired malfunctions) and the cost effectiveness of the completed procedure (measured by the ratio of the least expensive means of putting the equipment back into service while maintaining the lowest cost resulting from lost production). Thus you have three goals in effective electrical troubleshooting: speed, reliability, and cost effectiveness.

With a little thought, you should realize that merely learning a faster troubleshooting technique is not the entire answer to effectively getting equipment back into production. No troubleshooting technique can be set on automatic pilot—as a maintenance electrician, you need to rely on good judgment and knowledge in the way you use that technique. Your background of information on both the specific equipment you are troubleshooting and your general knowledge of the systems you are working with will have a significant bearing on how you conduct your troubleshooting procedure. The more background knowledge you have, the more apt you are to start closer to the actual problem you are looking for. More background knowledge will also increase your accuracy as you interpret your test results.

Individual learning patterns

Experience, of course, is an invaluable part of our learning experience. Most of us who work in the trades "learn through our hands." Much of what we are intuitively able to do is the result of having worked through similar problems while learning from those experiences.

However, experience is not the only method of effective learning. At some point, therefore, there must be a cautious balance between two rather opposite sources of information for the tradesperson. The first source of information is actual work experience. The second source of information is the acquisition of information through study. Simply stated, this means that a well-informed electrician is going to be involved in both types of learning activities; learning through actual work experiences and (particularly in the areas of expanding personal knowledge) through study.

It would be good at this point to clarify something I have just said. I purposely used the term "study." By using that term, however, I am not suggesting that this is necessarily an academic exercise. This book is not an education text, so I will avoid trying to analyze learning orientations. Nonetheless, as you are reading this chapter, you should be aware that I make quite a distinction between "learning" and the academic calisthenics we have all gone through in our formal education. I run the risk of generalization, but I think it is fair to say that most tradespeople learn best by conceptualizing a process as the first step rather than by rote memorization of the information before the application has been made. I think it is important for those of us who wish to be truly good electricians to accept the necessity of continued growth in our knowledge. That is not to say that each of us will gain knowledge in the same way. (Nonetheless, I think it is fair to assume, that at some point, gaining knowledge will involve reading. How the reading is done and how it is used—as with all learning—will become an individual matter.)

Technical training versus field experience

Technical (and particularly theoretical) information is often dismissed as being unnecessary for the field electrician. I strongly disagree! Our entire electrical profession is built around proper applications of some very sophisticated laws of energy physics. It is true that we may not need to understand all the formulas for conductance and resistivity in order to choose the correct wire and conduit size for a given load. Nonetheless, we will certainly be better electricians if we have a general concept of what is involved in these subjects. There can be more to doing a wiring job than following a table in the National Electrical Code (NEC); understanding why certain wire sizes are designated should be a part of what we bring to the trade.

Thus, the good electrician will have an understanding of the technical reasoning behind what is being done in the field just as the engineer must have an understanding of field procedures in order to do good design work. (Or stated in another way, I am no more impressed with the electrician who has never studied an electrical theory text than I am with the engineer who has never pulled a wire! They are both the poorer for their lack of additional knowledge or experience.)

Let me give you an example of the importance of understanding the theory of what we are doing in the field. I was troubleshooting a series of heater controllers on a large processing machine. When I got into the system, I found a strange concoction of wiring with improper lead wires used for the required J thermocouples. (There were even a few copper wire jumpers used where the thermocouple leads were too short.) Some electrician who preceded me had not done any homework on thermocouples; the same type of lead must run all the way from the controller to the thermocouple junction. (The two leads for J thermocouples are iron and copper-nickel.) No wonder the machine showed inaccurate readings. In spite of the time and expense required for the installation, its effectiveness was greatly reduced because the electrician didn't apply any knowledge of thermocouple connections.

I am trying to make a point. Your effectiveness as an electrical troubleshooter (measured by your speed and reliability and the cost effectiveness of your work) will often be determined by your knowledge of areas outside the immediate demands of your electrical license. Do you continue to study and learn in the field of electrical theory and practice? Do you go a step further and attempt to gain knowledge in outside, but related, fields to your work?

The need for you to effectively relate your electrical skills to knowledge in other areas is constant. In modern industrial equipment, the electrical system is frequently interrelated with other systems. You will be working with electrical control components in mechanical, hydraulic, refrigeration, and pneumatic systems. In addition you will be working with various process controls (heat, level indicators, proximity and counter sensors, etc.) which are integrated into complex machinery. A good troubleshooter must not only understand the electrical functions being tested but must also have a good working knowledge of any other systems encountered. That working knowledge includes not only the practical applications of these other systems, but their theory as well.

Choosing to Broaden Your Knowledge

Good electrical maintenance work, including the area of electrical troubleshooting, can become a much more challenging trade for the electrician who wants to take advantage of it. You can build on your skills as an electrician by systematically expanding your knowledge horizons into other technical areas. On the other hand, you can remain as "just an electrician." It's your choice.

I want you to look at three areas which offer significant potential for you as an electrician. Their value to you, however, will be determined by the kind of choices you make.

Advantages of trade licensing

As licensed electricians, we have a great advantage in the work area. For good safety reasons, the state has determined that electrical work can only be done by those who have appropriate levels of skill and knowledge. Each state has determined these knowledge and skill levels by testing and licensing. An electrician is free (legally, according to licensing law) to branch out into many other skill areas in plant maintenance. On the other hand, this same advantage is not available to others in the maintenance fields. Nonelectricians (again in terms of state electrical law) cannot do electrical work. In other words, where the job conditions merit, the electrician has many more options than anyone else in industrial maintenance. The electrician can be involved in many diverse areas of plant maintenance.

[I'd better clarify what I am trying to say or I will be in trouble. I am not suggesting that electricians make themselves obnoxious by taking others' jobs. And I am certainly not suggesting that we take on the

other unions in the maintenance department. I am merely aware of
the fact that many times we have significant latitude in our employment to broaden ourselves if we want. Though we will look at the potential advantages of working in a small shop later, this is by no
means the only area in which the electrician can broaden trade skills.
The large shop also has that potential. If you or I go into a large shop
with a willingness to learn from others—and with a nonthreatening
approach to their job security—we will usually be met more than half-
way. Acknowledge that a fellow employee knows more about his or
her trade than we do, and we will likely find a person who will be
happy to be our teacher. We can also reciprocate. With no violation of
the electrical code, we can become a source of information (when
desired!) of electrical safety and theory.]

Now, with the qualification of the preceding paragraph, I am suggesting that you have a significant advantage as a licensed electrician. In addition to the general mechanical skills in plant maintenance, there are a number of specialized skills which you could add to
your repertoire: refrigeration, hydraulics, pneumatics, and even welding and metal fabrication. What you do with this opportunity, however, will depend on your personal choice. If you wish to grow, the opportunity is always there, because it is more dependent on your
attitude than anything else.

Allow, however, for the fact that growth will take time. After all,
becoming an electrician was not something that you did overnight. So,
too, with other areas of knowledge. However, as you begin taking on
new challenges, you will see your competency increase. You will also
need to work carefully (and wisely, I might add!) with lead personnel
and/or management. Pace yourself so that your skills grow before you
aggressively take on jobs which are beyond your ability. (Irreparably
damaging expensive equipment will not encourage management to
give you the next job needing someone besides an electrician.)

You would be wise to consider your interest and ability for future
management positions. There is nothing "better" about the person
who eventually works into a management position than one who
spends an entire career in the applied trade. However, if you want to
move in the direction of management or some other form of further
responsibility as you get closer to retirement, you should plan toward
that goal now. Future management opportunities will undoubtedly be
conditioned by more than your skill as an electrician. You will certainly need management skills. (These skills may be evidenced by
nothing more than your ability to work with fellow employees. In
larger plants, however, the head office's evaluation of your management skills may actually be based on your willingness to enroll in
evening business courses.) In most cases, when opportunities are

given to a tradesperson to move into management, it will be based on that individual's broad range of technical ability and desire to learn.

The state has, in fact, given you as an electrician a decided advantage. It has given you an electrical license which allows you to work in an exclusive area without restricting your skill development in other trades. Taking advantage of that opportunity, however, is your responsibility and is dependent on the choices you make.

Advantages of small-shop employment

Every employment opportunity has its own advantages and disadvantages. Similarly, every employee is capable of utilizing a given set of circumstances to his or her best advantage, where another set of circumstances would be far less advantageous. Nonetheless, in my own experience, I have found that there are some significant benefits to working in a small shop if the employee is inclined to take advantage of them. (There are also disadvantages—lower pay and longer hours as a salaried employee are often among them.)

The most significant advantage in the small shop is a greater latitude of job opportunity. Typically, the small shop cannot cover each area of maintenance need with a specialist. Consequently, there is a great deal of overlap in the type of work done. If you want to broaden your work experience, then this setting will give you a greater opportunity to take on other maintenance responsibilities. The employer is faced with covering as broad a range of maintenance skills as possible with limited personnel. (In some cases, that may be an attempt at covering all maintenance needs with one qualified electrician.) If you are willing to work in other areas, the combination of an electrical license and your additional skills will put you in high demand. The uniqueness of the demands of the small shop will work both ways for you. Your broader skills will place you in higher demand in these employment settings. Equally, the small shop will give you an excellent place in which to develop broader skills simply because you will be the logical person to take on the job irrespective of your experience in that specific maintenance area.

There is a further consideration beyond just the skill development opportunities in the small shop, and that is the job status opportunity. The advancement progression in a large plant from maintenance electrician to plant manager may represent twenty or more years of seniority and a great deal of political savvy. In a small shop, it may be the same job. The real advantage, however, is seen in using the job as a basis for professional advancement. Let's use the example I just introduced. After three years of effective work in the above large plant, an electrician looking for other employment would be doing so as a low-ranking plant electrician with three years' experience (though possibly having excellent job references). On the other hand, the same electrician who had been the sole maintenance person in a small shop may quite legitimately represent him- or herself as a plant maintenance manager with three year's experience. That qualification may give the same electrician an opportunity for a maintenance manager position in a larger company. There are many reasons why a person may choose to stay in small-shop employment, but I am also suggesting that there is the very real opportunity for rapid professional advancement by spending time in carefully selected small-shop jobs.

Thus, you have some choices you can exercise in the type of employment you seek which can have an important bearing on your ultimate professional standing. Choosing the size of plant you wish to work in with the specific goal of broadening your knowledge and experience background can have significant benefits for you if you are careful and realistic in your planning.

Advantages of developing unique skills

Your personal marketability in the employment field will depend to a large extent on the unique skills you can bring to your employer. If you can bend conduit and pull wire like any other one of a thousand fellow electricians in your city, your marketability is no better than theirs; the competition will remain high for a limited number of jobs. On the other hand, if you can acquire unique skills which set you apart to a prospective employer, your job security and opportunities for advancement will greatly increase. The focus of this book is, of course, troubleshooting. Electrical troubleshooting is certainly a skill which will greatly enhance your professional advancement. In the next few paragraphs, I want you to gain an appreciation for some cause-and-effect relationships between the development of unique skills and effective troubleshooting.

You should have gathered by now that my personal philosophy of effective troubleshooting emphasizes your knowledge of the equipment you are working on. In addition to the electrical components, this will include mechanical, hydraulic, pneumatic, and whatever other systems are involved on the equipment. It is completely consistent with my understanding of the qualities of a good troubleshooting electrician, therefore, that I am suggesting in this section that you make it a habit to develop skills and knowledge in many areas outside the immediate field of electrical work.

In Chapter 6 I discussed the process of collecting information. The focus of that chapter was primarily the information pertinent to the particular machine breakdown at hand. Now, I want you to see other levels of information acquisition.

Specific equipment information.   First, there will be the in-depth information regarding the actual equipment you are working on. If you are in a plant maintenance position, this will include the entire range of the machinery in that plant. (Earlier, I used an example of a thermocouple problem that was the result of an electrician improperly wiring the leads. If you have thermocouple applications in your plant, then for you, this level of understanding would include a complete working knowledge of thermocouples and heat controllers. You should know how thermocouples work, the different types available for various heat ranges, the kinds of currents they generate, what the heat controller is sensing, how it is responding to the information, and so on. That kind of information is not a part of your electrical licensing, but it is the information which will give you the unique skills to effectively troubleshoot in a plant where thermocouples are used. Specific thermocouple knowledge may enable you to do a three-minute thermocouple repair by welding a new junction,[1] whereas a fellow electrician may shut the equipment down to replace the entire thermocouple and lead wire system.)

Your in-depth knowledge of the equipment in your plant will include a familiarization with maintenance and operation manuals for all of the equipment in the plant. You would want to learn machine functions well enough so that you can operate the equipment without depending on machine operators. You should also become familiar with systems represented on the machines in your plant. (Hydraulic equipment is an important example. This is the reason for the closing chapter, Troubleshooting Hydraulic Systems.)

Broad information.   Second, there will be the broader information level which will go beyond equipment in your plant. As you develop in this area, you will find to your amazement that there are many alternate ways to do things besides the way it is done in your plant (and possibly, besides the way it is done in your particular industry). There are often good reasons why certain conventions are followed in a given plant, and they should not be changed carelessly. But don't always assume that it represents the only or the best way to accomplish the task. Many times a piece of equipment (or control devices on the equipment) was installed the way it was because it represented technology at the time of installation—or possibly it was the result of a low-bid installation. From that time on, however, all repairs have been done as though each component item represented an optimum standard in the industry and great care has been taken to replace de-

---

[1] A thermocouple junction is nothing more than a fusion of the two dissimilar leads.

fective components with exact equivalent replacement parts. During equipment repair, systems can often be upgraded for more reliable performance with alternate replacement components. Upgrading equipment, however, will require specialized and broad knowledge on the part of someone doing the work. The electrician who has taken time to broaden his or her range of knowledge in these areas will bring an employer some valuable assets. These unique knowledge skills become not only the basis of better troubleshooting, but they add significantly to job security and advancement potential.

What has been said of knowledge skills could just as well be said of any number of work skills. The more the electrician understands and can do, the greater will be the job opportunities which become available for that person. Equally, that greater skill is going to make a substantial contribution to increased troubleshooting effectiveness.

Each of these three areas (the advantages of trade licensing, the advantage of a small-shop setting, and the advantages of developing higher skill levels) are all ultimately concerned with increasing your ability in troubleshooting. Each of them represents an area in which you can develop skills beyond the basic skills of the general electrician. These skills can dramatically increase your troubleshooting speed by helping you locate problem areas as you work your way through an inoperative piece of equipment.

Tools for Broadening Your Knowledge

Broadening your knowledge—which should make you both a better troubleshooter and a better electrician—will not take place simply because you are working in the trade. It will be the result of a planned learning approach on your part. (I do not want to overlook the fact that each of us learns differently. Therefore, you will need to adapt what I am saying to your own needs. Nonetheless, be realistic. If your study methods are not producing substantial growth in knowledge, then you need to reevaluate what you are doing. Ultimately, however, if you do achieve the competency in your field that this broader knowledge can bring to you, it will take place because you were willing to do the hard work to get there.) I would suggest the following areas of effort as being the most productive in helping you reach your goal:

Reading.   Some form of consistent reading is mandatory if you wish to acquire significant knowledge in the trades. In addition to specific technical information dealing with your immediate electrical trade concerns, I would also suggest broad reading in many other areas. Your best ideas will often be based on information from entirely different application sources. Further, an understanding of other subjects may give you insight into the current problems you are dealing with. (I could give many illustrations. For example, understanding the process used in the manufacture of solid-state devices may have little immediate application in your plant. Yet, your background in that area may prevent future equipment downtime by prompting you to use a better heat sink or a varistor when installing a solid-state device.)

Wisely selecting your reading materials will be as important as the time spent in reading. Books and magazines will always be important sources of reading material. In addition, do not overlook what is available through equipment suppliers in their technical bulletins and catalogs. There is a genius to the way this material is condensed and organized. Four or five pages in the technical section of an equipment catalog may give the entire contents of an engineering text in summary form. For a brief acquaintance with a wide range of subjects, technical catalogs and bulletins are an invaluable source of information. (While you have the catalog in hand, study the main sections as well. Familiarization with the equipment available on the market may be a help to you later when you are upgrading or altering electrical equipment.)

Work experience.   Don't overlook the learning opportunities you have in your regular work. This is particularly true when you purposefully attempt work in new areas. Your attitude, however, is an important part of whether or not this adds to your knowledge. Some electricians can spend their time going through the motions and gain little by the experience. On the other hand, if you will be open to information which is available to you through that experience, it can become an important part of your learning activity. (Learning to ask appropriate questions can be an important source of information. We are continually around other people in the trades who know things we don't. Fellow tradespersons and equipment suppliers can give you an amazing amount of new information.)

Seminars and continuing education.   These sources of information must be carefully evaluated; some are far too expensive for the value of the information given. (Some are just plain worthless, having little benefit beyond the coffee and cinnamon rolls!) Nonetheless, there are many things available which are well worth the expense and time. (Many excellent seminars are provided at no cost by equipment suppliers. These seminars may often be the basis of very applicable information for your particular plant maintenance needs. You can frequently question a competent seminar leader who would be worth many dollars if hired as a consultant.)

You will also want to investigate adult continuing education programs. There are an increasing number of trade classes being offered through local community colleges. As these programs develop, more specialized types of information are being offered. In addition to the electrical code classes, you can often find excellent courses in motor controls, solid-state devices, plant maintenance, programmable controllers, etc. Most colleges with trades classes also offer other related areas of interest to electricians such as refrigeration, heating systems, and the like. Many of these classes are offered in the evenings.

Equipment examination. In Chapter 6, Collecting Information, you were encouraged to examine equipment after it fails. Take that a step further, trying to think through both the principles of operation of that piece of equipment or component, and then look for the reasons why it failed from the standpoint of electrical theory. (Why, for instance, did a motor burn out because the voltage dropped? The coils evidence the same charring as if the motor had run on too high a voltage. The answer is not in merely looking at the motor. It is in understanding the effects of heat produced by overcurrent, which can be a product of either a high- or a low-voltage condition—depending, of course, on the motor's load.)[2]

Advanced licensing. An excellent way to increase your understanding of electrical problems is to continually work toward advanced licenses. Not only will advanced licenses enhance your job opportunities, but they will be a significant means of upgrading your electrical knowledge.

A Closing Thought

Why has so much attention been given to the subject of learning in a troubleshooting text? It has been done for a very basic reason. Troubleshooting is, by nature, an attempt at finding a yet unknown malfunction. (The malfunction may not even be electrical.) In the final anal-

---

[2] In Chapter 8 you were given a horsepower formula for a three-phase motor. By studying the formula you will realize that electrical power is derived from two components (volts × amps or watts). If a motor is supplied with a lower-than-normal voltage, and if the power output (horsepower) can proportionately drop (as in the case of a blade fan), the current could remain approximately the same. In this case, the motor would not be in jeopardy. On the other hand, if the voltage dropped but the motor power output remained constant (as, for example, with a loaded conveyor belt), the motor amperage would need to rise proportionately to maintain the same horsepower. If the current rises, the motor coils will be subject to additional heat. So too, if the voltage rises (as in the case of the VOM coil mentioned in Chapter 5), the current will be proportional to the voltage. Thus, either a high or a low voltage could result in a burned-out motor if the load was constant in the low-voltage condition.

ysis, there are really only two approaches to isolating the problem. The least effective method is to start at the beginning of the circuit and check everything as it comes until the electrical malfunction is found. The efficient approach is to determine the most likely area of malfunction and confine testing to that precise area.

How does an electrician determine the most likely area of malfunction? Obviously, that determination is dependent on the electrician's understanding of the equipment being tested. The more completely the equipment is understood—and the more information the electrician possesses about the total range of systems involved—the more effective the troubleshooting process will be.

The purpose of this book is to teach you an effective troubleshooting technique. On-line troubleshooting can save you a great deal of downtime. However, it is not the rote use of the technique which will produce results. Effective results will only be achieved by the electrician who has an appropriate background of knowledge in conjunction with the skills to use the troubleshooting technique.

Therefore, if you want to become an effective troubleshooter, you will need to learn the troubleshooting technique as well as orient yourself to understanding the equipment you are working on. That will best be achieved if you work toward broadening your understanding of all aspects of the equipment on which you are working.

There is much that you can do in the electrical trades beyond troubleshooting. Greater professional effectiveness and responsibility, however, will demand broadening of your skills and knowledge.

Chapter Review

Effective troubleshooting is measured by three important components: the speed of the troubleshooting process (measured as the total machinery downtime), the reliability of the diagnosis and repair (measured by the absence of future downtime caused by undiagnosed or poorly repaired malfunctions), and cost effectiveness (measured by the ratio of the least expensive means of putting the equipment back into service while at the same time maintaining the lowest cost from lost production).

Since effective troubleshooting is more than a problem-solving technique, it follows that the electrician will need to apply broad knowledge and judgment in order to accomplish the task. A background of technical information will greatly contribute to the effectiveness of the troubleshooting process. Though field experience is an important part of the electrician's learning process, it is by no means the only area of concentration. An appropriate study of practical and theoretical written material should be a part of the electrician's plan for skill improvement.

The work context can make an important contribution to the electrician's overall knowledge. Of the many work-related ways in which broader background knowledge can be gained, three were mentioned. Electrical trade licensing gives the electrician the unique opportunity of developing multiple trade skills without violating code and safety requirements. Employment in a small shop may give the electrician opportunity to gain background in numerous mechanical and hydraulic areas. The electrician should be consciously aware of the advantage of developing unique skills in any employment or avocation situation.

The electrician should have a planned learning approach to the information available in the trade fields. Acquisition of new information will come in many forms. Reading, work experience, seminars and continuing education, equipment examination, and advanced licensing were mentioned as areas worthy of attention.

The need for greater knowledge and learning has been emphasized in this electrical troubleshooting text because, by its very nature, troubleshooting is an attempt at finding a malfunction which is outside the normal electrical circuit function. The skill of the troubleshooting electrician will be highly dependent on an ability to appropriately use information to isolate unknown fault areas.

Chapter Questions

Thinking through the text

1. What are the three parts of the effective troubleshooting process? Can you give a brief description of each?

2. What advantage is gained in electrical troubleshooting through possessing greater background knowledge?

3. What advantage does the licensed electrician gain over other plant maintenance personnel?

4. According to the viewpoint of this chapter, what specific benefits are to be found in reading?

5. Can you explain how the examination of failed equipment is a part of the electrician's learning experience?

6. In what way can advanced licensing contribute to more effective electrical troubleshooting?

7. Troubleshooting is, by its very nature, an attempt at finding an unknown variable in the electrical circuit. How does greater knowledge on the part of the troubleshooting electrician aid in diagnostic work?

Deepening your electrical understanding

8. Speed, reliability, and cost effectiveness are interrelated parts of effective troubleshooting. Speed is probably the simplest concept of the three to un

Troubleshooting
Hydraulic Systems

*In this chapter you will be given a brief
introduction to hydraulic systems and their
troubleshooting. This will be done by showing you
how to read a hydraulic print and by giving you a
brief explanation of the functions of various
hydraulic controls and actuators. Specific attention
will be given to electrical controls. A final section
will give you an overview of hydraulic systems.*

Why should an electrician study hydraulics? The answer will, of course, depend on your specific job. Nonetheless, if you are working in any kind of manufacturing plant, there is a high probability that you will be servicing electrical systems which are controlling hydraulic equipment. Your value as both a general maintenance electrician and a troubleshooter will be greatly enhanced if you understand basic hydraulic systems.

How involved you eventually become with hydraulic maintenance is a decision you alone will make. I personally feel that there is a great demand in industry for the electrician who can cover a wide range of maintenance tasks. My purpose in this chapter, however, is not to give a course in hydraulic repair. It is merely to give enough information so that you can knowledgeably troubleshoot the electrical system on a hydraulic-actuated piece of equipment.[1]

---

[1] If you are interested in further study of hydraulics, I would suggest the *Industrial Hydraulics Manual* published by Vickers. (Vickers, Inc., P.O. Box 302, Troy, MI 48007-0302. The book is often available through Vickers' hydraulic dealerships.) This book is an excellent source of information with numerous illustrations. Although very complete, the book is easy to follow whether you are just beginning in hydraulics or are quite familiar with the subject.

Hydraulic Diagrams

Before actually looking at specific hydraulic symbols, I want to give you an orientation to what you will see on hydraulic prints. If you are not familiar with hydraulic diagrams, look at the diagram in Appendix B. The hydraulic diagram is a pictorial representation of the fluid circuit. The hydraulic circuit is represented by four broad symbolic categories.

Pumps. You will always see a pump system on a hydraulic circuit. Conventionally, it is at the bottom of the drawing.

Lines. The diagram will show the rigid supply lines and hoses as lines on the drawing. The lines are not labeled with numbers or letters as they are in electrical drawings. However, their physical location in relationship to the components they are serving identifies their function.

Valves. All hydraulic systems are controlled by valves. There is a wide range of valve functions, from controlling set pressures to determining the direction of flow. Valves may be manually, electrically, mechanically, or pressure operated. You should also be aware that there are two important valve functions (direct operation and pilot operation). In some cases where the hydraulic volume is small, a direct-acting valve arrangement can be used. (Refer to valve 44 in Appendix B.) In this valve, the electrically operated valve is used to control the actual hydraulic fluid circuit to the actuator (the motor or cylinder).
   However, in most cases, the hydraulic fluid volume requires a larger valve than could practically be controlled by an electric solenoid. (Refer to valves 18, 19, or 20 in Appendix B.) In this arrangement a pilot valve is used. An electrical solenoid-operated valve (this is the pilot valve) is used to control a small-volume hydraulic circuit. The small-volume hydraulic circuit in turn controls the main valve. The main valve is thus *hydraulically,* not electrically, operated.

Actuators. Generally, the hydraulic fluid is acting against either a hydraulic motor or a cylinder. The hydraulic motor produces rotary motion, whereas the hydraulic cylinder produces linear motion. All hydraulic systems can be visualized as producing one or the other motions. Motors and cylinders are called actuators.
   If you are not yet familiar with hydraulic diagrams, you should have no difficulty in quickly learning how to read them. Once you understand the meaning of each of the symbols, you will then merely trace the circuit to understand its function.

However, there is one area of explanation which is necessary in order to avoid confusion. You will later see a component enclosure symbol (it is a box drawn with a broken line). The symbol merely indicates the location or physical grouping of the valve(s) or component(s). It means that the valve(s) is enclosed or is a part of an assembly so that it will form a unit rather than individual components. The important distinction is that the lines do not represent hydraulic circuits. (If you refer to Appendix B, you will see a broken-line box drawn around valves 18, 19, and 20. These lines indicate that the three valves are enclosed inside of the equipment or they are mounted as two valves in a single unit—component enclosure lines are not hydraulic circuit lines.) Notice that the entire center portion of the drawing is also enclosed in a broken-line box (valves 18, 19, 20, 23, 24, 8, and a number of individual valves and lines). Again, this box indicates a physical location, not a hydraulic circuit.

Hydraulic Symbols

Table 12.1 gives the definitions of some of the most commonly used hydraulic symbols. These symbols conform to the specifications of the American National Standards Institute (ANSI).

Because this is merely an overview of hydraulics, I am not going to explain each symbol. The following brief explanations, however, will deal with some of the less obvious symbol meanings.

Line functions

1. *Working lines* are the main lines carrying fluid to or from the pumps and actuators.

2. *Pilot lines* are the control lines which carry the hydraulic fluid from a control (pilot) valve to a high-volume main valve. (Generally, these are passages drilled in the mounting blocks—they are not pipes or hoses.)

3. *Drain lines* are used to carry nonworking (low-pressure) hydraulic fluid back to the tank.

4. *Flexible lines* are usually high-pressure, steel-reinforced, rubber-jacketed hose. This is in contrast to rigid lines, which are usually steel pipe.

5. *Restricted lines* (which are either fixed or adjustable) are used to limit the travel speed of a cylinder or motor by limiting the flow (but not the pressure) of the hydraulic supply line. (In actuality, this is a hydraulic component rather than a physical line, although it is represented as a line function.)

TABLE 12.1

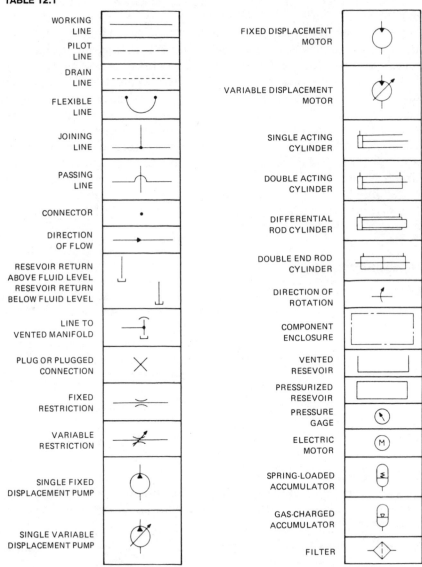

WORKING LINE	FIXED DISPLACEMENT MOTOR
PILOT LINE	
DRAIN LINE	VARIABLE DISPLACEMENT MOTOR
FLEXIBLE LINE	
JOINING LINE	SINGLE ACTING CYLINDER
PASSING LINE	DOUBLE ACTING CYLINDER
CONNECTOR	DIFFERENTIAL ROD CYLINDER
DIRECTION OF FLOW	
RESEVOIR RETURN ABOVE FLUID LEVEL	DOUBLE END ROD CYLINDER
RESEVOIR RETURN BELOW FLUID LEVEL	DIRECTION OF ROTATION
LINE TO VENTED MANIFOLD	COMPONENT ENCLOSURE
PLUG OR PLUGGED CONNECTION	VENTED RESEVOIR
FIXED RESTRICTION	PRESSURIZED RESEVOIR
	PRESSURE GAGE
VARIABLE RESTRICTION	ELECTRIC MOTOR
SINGLE FIXED DISPLACEMENT PUMP	SPRING-LOADED ACCUMULATOR
	GAS-CHARGED ACCUMULATOR
SINGLE VARIABLE DISPLACEMENT PUMP	FILTER

Adapted from INDUSTRIAL HYDRAULICS MANUAL, Vickers Inc., Troy, Michigan. Used by permission.

Pumps.   Hydraulic pumps supply hydraulic fluid to the actuators in the system. Pumps are either fixed- or variable-displacement units. A fixed-displacement pump has a given output volume for a given motor speed. The displacement of a variable pump can be controlled to give

TABLE 12.1 (Continued)

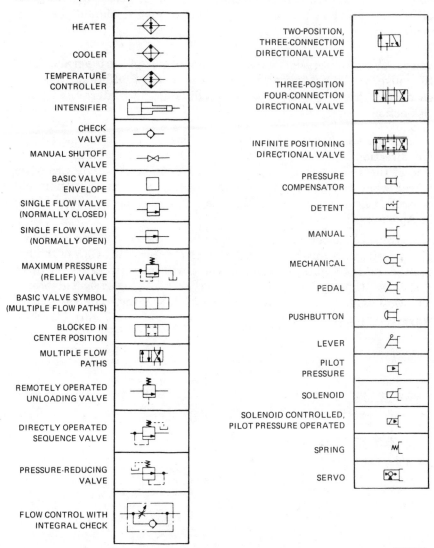

HEATER		TWO-POSITION, THREE-CONNECTION DIRECTIONAL VALVE	
COOLER		THREE-POSITION FOUR-CONNECTION DIRECTIONAL VALVE	
TEMPERATURE CONTROLLER		INFINITE POSITIONING DIRECTIONAL VALVE	
INTENSIFIER		PRESSURE COMPENSATOR	
CHECK VALVE		DETENT	
MANUAL SHUTOFF VALVE		MANUAL	
BASIC VALVE ENVELOPE		MECHANICAL	
SINGLE FLOW VALVE (NORMALLY CLOSED)		PEDAL	
SINGLE FLOW VALVE (NORMALLY OPEN)		PUSHBUTTON	
MAXIMUM PRESSURE (RELIEF) VALVE		LEVER	
BASIC VALVE SYMBOL (MULTIPLE FLOW PATHS)		PILOT PRESSURE	
BLOCKED IN CENTER POSITION		SOLENOID	
MULTIPLE FLOW PATHS		SOLENOID CONTROLLED, PILOT PRESSURE OPERATED	
REMOTELY OPERATED UNLOADING VALVE		SPRING	
DIRECTLY OPERATED SEQUENCE VALVE		SERVO	
PRESSURE-REDUCING VALVE			
FLOW CONTROL WITH INTEGRAL CHECK			

varying output volumes depending on need (though the motor is running at a constant speed). (The variable pump is used as an energy-saving device.) A directional arrow (which indicates the inlet and outlet sides of the pump) may or may not be used in the hydraulic schematic.

Actuators. Actuators are the mechanical components which convert hydraulic flow to mechanical motion. They are either motors (rotary motion) or cylinders (linear motion). Though there are a number of different cylinder configurations, the symbols should be self-explanatory.

Valves. Valves represent the most complex part of the diagram. Since the valve can be drawn to represent a number of different functions, each valve drawing must be studied individually to determine its precise action.

1. *Check valves* are used as one-way valves; the fluid will flow in one direction but cannot return (or cannot go from the high-pressure side of the system to the low-pressure side). Check valves are often paired with restricting valves to give full flow in one direction and controlled flow in the reverse direction. (See the example in valve 25 in Appendix B.)

2. *Valve envelopes* are used to indicate the function of the valve in a given position. A directional valve is used to direct the flow of the hydraulic fluid. A typical directional valve will have either two or three positions. (However, it is identified as either a two-way valve or a four-way valve because of the number of flow paths.) The valve is always drawn in its center—or rest—position. (Refer to Figure 12.1 for a

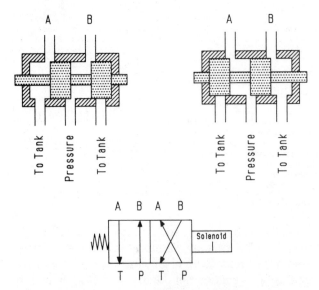

Figure 12.1 A typical two-way hydraulic directional valve (valve 41 with solenoid I from the hydraulic diagram in Appendix B is shown). The left and right sectional drawings (*top*) are represented by the left and right graphic symbols (*bottom*), respectively.

drawing of a typical two-way directional control valve, and Figure 12.2 for a drawing of a typical four-way directional control valve.) The valve envelopes are the flow paths for that valve for each of its two or three positions.

The valve is drawn so that you see the flow path when the valve is in its relaxed position. (In many cases, that position will be blocked so that there is no flow. The symbol for a blocked valve port is a capped line drawn like a T.) To visualize the flow path in other positions, you need to mentally move the envelope to the other position(s). For an example, refer to Figure 12.2. In the center position there is no flow. When solenoid U is energized, the valve will shift to the right-hand envelope, which will result in a straight-through fluid flow. If solenoid V is energized, the valve will shift to the left-hand envelope and the fluid flow will be reversed. The two-way valve in Figure 12.1 will direct flow from the pressure port P through port B. The fluid will return to the tank through port A. When solenoid I is energized, the flow will be reversed.

In order to avoid confusion you must remember that only one envelope is operational at any one time. The number of envelopes for a given valve shows the number of working positions in which that valve is capable of operating. To understand each of the various flow

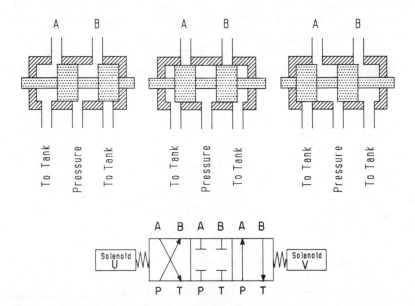

Figure 12.2   A typical four-way hydraulic directional control valve (valve 44 with solenoids U and V from the hydraulic diagram is shown). The left, center, and right sectional drawings (*top*) are represented by the left, center, and right graphic symbols (*bottom*), respectively.

paths for that valve you must mentally shift the valve to its other envelope positions.

3. *Valve operation* is designated with a symbol outside of the envelope. Electrical solenoid operation has already been mentioned. Other symbols would indicate that the control valve is manually operated, has spring centering or return, or has some other specialized form of operation.

Most hydraulic diagrams will number the components (such as valves and pumps). You will then find a legend section on the diagram which will identify each of the components by the diagram number. Typically, the information which is given includes the valve function, the valve replacement numbers, and the pressure settings or other pertinent operating information. Study the legend section of the hydraulic diagram in Appendix B.

Troubleshooting with a Hydraulic Diagram

The hydraulic diagram can give very useful information for general troubleshooting as well as specific electrical troubleshooting. I want to show you a brief example of how that might work in both cases.

In Chapter 7 you were working with the ejector system on the ladder diagram (solenoid I on line 34). Now, let's see how the hydraulic diagram could help you. In both of the following examples the ejector system is not functioning.

As was the case in the example in Chapter 7, you are again told that there is a problem with one of the molding machines in the production area. The ejection system is not functioning. In this case, however, it will not function in any mode. (If you remember, in the previous example the ejection system would work in the manual setting but not in the automatic mode.)

Again, you make a preliminary visual equipment and safety check and find nothing wrong. This time, however, the machine has not been in production. The condition is different in that the setup person from the last shift started changing the die, but left the job to be completed by your shift's setup crew. The machine is ready to operate, with the exception of the ejection cycle, which does not function.

Using the hydraulic diagram to locate electrical components. In the previous examples, you located the circuit diagram lines you needed to work on from the electrical diagram itself. In this case, however, you have a copy of the hydraulic diagram with you. Therefore, as a first step in your electrical work, you start with the hydraulic diagram. (Refer to the hydraulic diagram in Appendix B.) On the upper portion of the drawing you locate the ejector cylinder. Since the cylinder is not extending, you know that the critical line is the one drawn as entering the closed end of the cylinder. (That is, of the two lines supplying the ejector cylinder, the line you will want to check is the one drawn on the left of the cylinder symbol.)

You trace the line through the entire circuit and discover only two control areas between the cylinder and the pump. The first is valve 41 which is controlled by solenoid I (ejector). The second is control valve 42.

Since you are doing your electrical testing first, you now know that you need to verify the operation of solenoid I. (As you recall from the procedure in the previous illustration, there are two solenoids on which the operation of the ejector cylinder is dependent. The first solenoid is I, which you have just identified. The second solenoid is J—ejector pressure. Solenoid J is at the lower right-hand corner of the diagram. If you are adept at reading hydraulic diagrams, you will see how this controls the line pressure by shifting to pressure-relief valve 36. For the present example, however, it may be easier for you to locate the solenoids in the circuit from the electrical diagram.)

In the same way as you have done before, you have the operator run the machine until it stalls on the ejection cycle. Since you have identified solenoid I (ejector) from the hydraulic diagram as being the checkpoint, you locate that solenoid on the ladder diagram and proceed with a voltage check on the wire leading to the solenoid.

If your first voltage test indicates an electrical problem, you will continue working with the electrical system. However, for the sake of this illustration, you find that the electrical system is fully operational. Now you will need to check the hydraulic system itself.

Using the hydraulic diagram for component checking. When you trace the lines from the ejector cylinder to the pump, you notice that there are two control areas. The first control is valve 42 which is labeled as the throttle check valve. (In other words, this valve is a manual speed-control valve.)

Logic says that something could be wrong with valve 42. When you check the valve you discover that for some reason, it has been turned to its closed position. (The setup person from the last shift apparently made the adjustment and said nothing to the next shift. It is not an adjustment which is frequently changed and it was overlooked as a possible cause of the ejector malfunction.) Opening the valve and recycling the machine will indicate that the problem is solved.

Depending on what the actual cause of the problem had been, you could have used the hydraulic diagram to help you locate an area for electrical testing or to locate specific hydraulic components which need testing. Certainly not all hydraulic testing will be this simple. Yet, you would be surprised at how many times both hydraulic and electrical problems are simply and quickly solved if you can use diagram information to isolate the probable problem areas.

Before leaving this example, did you notice the component enclosure lines drawn around valves 41, 42, and the other valves nearby? (Refer to Appendix B.) Those lines are not to be read as part of the hydraulic circuit—there is no connection (other than through the main supply lines) between the individual circuits in the enclosure.

Electrical Problems in the Hydraulic System

Your initial task in troubleshooting a hydraulic system is to determine if the problem is an electrical control problem or a hydraulic problem. (See Fig. 12.3.) As a rule of thumb, if the hydraulic circuit completely fails to function, it is an electrical problem. On the other hand, erratic, slow, or noisy operation—or the presence of excessive heat or leaks—is an indication that the problem is in the hydraulic part of the system. By far the higher percentage of problems will be in the electrical controls.

In earlier chapters, the subject of troubleshooting control components has been adequately discussed. The one remaining area which you will occasionally need to work with is the solenoid coil. In Chapter 9 you were told how to use a clamp-on ammeter for coil testing. That test procedure will supply valuable information when you work with coils. It will allow you to determine if the solenoid is failing to mechanically shift (which would indicate a mechanical problem with the valve itself). If the current draw is high, indicating that the spool valve is not shifting, the valve will require mechanical repair.

Generally, a problem with the solenoid coil will require either a simple lead wire repair or replacing the coil. You will occasionally find loose connections on the coil terminals. This is especially true if wire nuts are used and the terminals have been reconnected a number of times. After tightening the connections another check should be done to verify the system. If, however, a continuity check of the coil shows any fault, the coil should be replaced. For the most part, coils will give long service, but when they evidence shorting or deterioration, there is nothing which can be done in order to salvage them—they should be replaced.

In the next section you will see some general guidelines which can be used for checking the actual hydraulic system.

Figure 12.3 This is an actual test of a hydraulic solenoid valve done from the electrical panel. (Solenoid P on the ladder diagram is being checked by measuring the current on wire 50.) The time savings of this testing procedure over physically dismantling the actual valve should be obvious.

Overview of Hydraulic Systems[2]

General introduction to hydraulic systems

The information given in this overview section is generally true for any hydraulic system. However, when troubleshooting or repairing a specific hydraulic system, information from the equipment supplier may be needed.

System design

When working on hydraulic systems, it is best to assume that the original system as designed by the manufacturer was properly engineered for its intended service. At times, field modifications will be required because of the addition of new functions or because replacement parts for

---

[2] The information in this section is adapted from the 1986 equipment catalog published by Nickerson Machinery Company, Accord, Massachusetts. Nickerson Machinery Company supplies after-market plastic processing equipment which includes hydraulic component replacement parts.

that specific machine are no longer available. However, a seemingly uncomplicated procedure such as relocating a subsystem or changing a component part can cause unexpected problems. Because of the need to keep all repairs and modifications within the engineering parameters of the original design, the following suggestions should be kept in mind:

1. Each component part in the hydraulic circuit must be compatible with the entire integrated system. For example, if you are replacing or adding an inlet filter on the pump, it must be adequately sized to handle the flow rate of the system. Failure to match the filter to the flow rate could cause cavitation and subsequent damage to the pump.

2. All lines must be properly sized and be free of restrictive bends. Undersized or restricted lines may result in decreased equipment performance because of reduced flow rates.

3. Some components must be mounted in specific positions relative to other parts of the system. Modifications may jeopardize the performance of the hydraulic system. For example, the housing of an in-line pump must be lower than the fluid level in the hydraulic reservoir. The pump housing must remain full of hydraulic fluid in order to provide proper lubrication when the pump is started.

4. The addition of adequate test points for pressure readings, although not essential for operation, will reduce troubleshooting time. Permanently mounted gauges or quick-disconnect fittings for portable gauges allow faster evaluation of the system's performance.

Familiarity with the system

Knowing the operation of the specific hydraulic system you will be troubleshooting is probably the greatest aid to fast and effective diagnostic work. Every component in the system has a purpose. The construction and operating characteristics of each should be understood. For example, knowing that a solenoid-controlled directional valve can be manually actuated may save considerable time in isolating a defective solenoid.

In addition to the general operation of any given hydraulic system, the following specific items are areas of information you should have available to you when you are troubleshooting a faulty hydraulic system:

1. You should know the capabilities of the specific system you are working on. Each component in the system has a maximum rated speed, torque, or pressure. Loading the system beyond the specified limits greatly increases the possibility of system failure and hazard.

2. You should know the correct operating pressures. The overall hydraulic system will have a maximum set pressure, as will individual subsystems. For example, the pressure-relief valve for the entire system may be set at 2,200 psi, while an individual hydraulic motor in the system may have a maximum operating pressure of only 1,500 psi and will be controlled by its own pressure-relief valve. Always set and check pressures with gauges—do not rely on guesswork for high-limit pressure settings.

A complete hydraulic schematic should include the set pressures for each pressure-relief valve in the system. In cases where specific pressure settings are not specified on the drawings, the following procedure may be used to set secondary relief valves.

Be certain that the main pressure-relief valve(s) are set at the specified pressure limit. (Under no circumstances should a secondary relief valve be set at a higher pressure than the main system relief valves.) Reduce the secondary relief valve to its lowest pressure and energize the hydraulic system. (The system will generally stall.) Increase the set pressure until the system operates normally. The correct operating pressure is the lowest pressure which will allow adequate performance of the system. It must, however, be a pressure below the maximum ratings of the machine and within the operating ranges of the hydraulic components.

3. You should know the proper signal levels if you are servicing servo-control systems. (Servo valves are infinitely positioned valves. Unlike a conventional spool valve which controls only the direction of the fluid, the servo valve can control the amount as well as the direction of the fluid. Thus, the valve can be used to control the position, speed, or acceleration of an actuator if the appropriate feedback sensing devices are included in the electrical circuit.) Troubleshooting servo-control systems will include hydraulic and electronic troubleshooting skills. You should also be aware that servo systems are much less tolerant of hydraulic oil contamination than conventional pilot-operated spool-valve systems.

Develop systematic procedures

As is the case in any troubleshooting work, you need to begin by carefully observing the system. Component failures may often be identified by either abnormalities evident in the component itself, or by a characteristic action of the hydraulic system. A humming or noisy solenoid valve indicates a jammed or nonfunctioning spool. A creeping hydraulic cylinder indicates worn piston packings or possibly leaking control or check valves. Develop a logical sequence for setting valves, mechanical stops, interlocks, and electrical controls. Start with the parts of the system which have the greatest influence on the entire system. (In other words, if there is a pressure problem in a cylinder, check the main pressure-relief valves if the line pressure is low, rather than starting with the assumption that the failure is in the cylinder itself.) Tracing of flow paths can often be accomplished by listening for flow in the lines or feeling them for warmth.

Recognize indications of failure

The ability to quickly identify component failures in a specific system is usually acquired with experience. However, the following indicators are usually a sign of impending failure:

Excessive heat. Excessive heat indicates abnormal conditions. Heat may be the result of electrical, hydraulic, mechanical, or heat-exchanger problems. Hydraulic problems often generate heat. For example, a warmer-than-normal tank return line on a relief valve indicates continuous operation at the relief valve setting pressure. Hydraulic fluids which have a low viscosity will increase the internal leakage of components, resulting in a heat rise. Cavitation and slippage in a pump will also generate heat. Mechanical problems may also generate heat. A misaligned motor coupling places an excessive load on the bearings and can be readily identified by the heat generated.

Excessive noise. Excessive noise indicates wear, misalignment, or cavitation (which is air in the fluid). Contaminated fluid can cause a relief valve to stick and chatter. Pump noises (usually caused by cavitation) can be caused by dirty filters or fluid, high fluid viscosity (because it is cold or the wrong grade), excessive drive speed, low reservoir level, loose intake lines (which allow air into the fluid), or actual mechanical problems such as a worn pump or coupling.

Practice appropriate maintenance

Three simple maintenance procedures have the greatest effect on hydraulic system performance, efficiency, and life. Yet, the very simplicity of them may be the reason they are so often overlooked.

1. Maintain clean hydraulic fluid of the proper type and viscosity in the reservoir. Keep the level within the normal operating range.

2. Change filters and clean strainers at appropriate intervals.

3. Keep all connections tight and leak-free, eliminating air inclusion in the hydraulic fluid.

Work safely

Safe working practices are mandatory during hydraulic maintenance and troubleshooting just as they are in electrical troubleshooting. In addition to the precautions you take against electrical hazard, you will also need to be aware of the unique safety requirements of the hydraulic equipment. Again, as stressed in Chapter 1, good judgment is probably the most important factor in overall hydraulic safety. Keep your hands away from moving (or potentially moving) equipment. Don't manually override hydraulic pilot valves unless you have set the machine so that it can operate safely. Be aware that most hydraulic fluids are flammable.

Aside from the hazards inherent with moving machinery, probably the greatest danger area related to hydraulic equipment is the presence of fluid under high pressure. The system used for the illustrations in this chapter is set for 2,000 psi on the main lines. (Look at the legend section of the diagram in Appendix B. Valves 1, 3, and 5 are set at 2,000 psi working pressure.) At these pressures, bursting lines or fittings can become lethal. Never put your hand in front of a leak—the fluid can penetrate the skin and cause severe damage.

Never adjust a pressure-relief valve to a higher setting with the motor off. Set the pressure with the system in operation and watch a pressure gauge while you make the adjustments. This prevents the system from surpassing its upper limits. (This caution comes as a result of an unforgettable experience. I was rebuilding the hydraulic system on a large hydraulically operated machine which had a maximum working pressure of 2,200 psi. I had replaced a number of valves, including the main pressure-relief valve. I mounted a quick-disconnect fitting and gauge on the valve to set the pressures. When the installation was complete, I started the motor from the panel and then walked to the back of the machine to look at the gauge. In the time it took me to realize what I was seeing, the gauge moved from 2,900 to over 3,000 psi and was still climbing. I don't think I have ever moved as fast as I did then, racing from the back of the machine to the big red button on the operator's panel! That was the last relief valve I ever installed without first backing the pressure screw to the lowest setting.)

Appendix E gives a complete hydraulic troubleshooting guide.

Chapter Review

A basic understanding of hydraulic systems may greatly enhance your value as a maintenance electrician. If nothing else, the knowledge will help you work more effectively when you are troubleshooting electrical controls on hydraulic equipment.

The hydraulic diagram is a pictorial representation of the hydraulic system. It will include symbols for pumps, lines, valves, and actuators (which are either hydraulic motors or cylinders). A typical hydraulic diagram will identify valves (usually with numbers) with a legend on the side. However, the hydraulic supply lines (or hoses) have no specific identification markings; it is necessary to visually trace each line to determine its function.

Hydraulic flow control valves are used to control the direction of the hydraulic fluid. A specialized symbol called an envelope is used to designate each of the flow possibilities for a given valve. The envelope is shown on the drawing in its relaxed (nonactuated) position. To determine the other flow patterns, the adjacent envelopes are mentally moved into their operational position(s). Flow control valves are generally either two-way valves (valves with two positions and two flow paths) or four-way valves (valves with three positions and four flow paths).

The hydraulic diagram may be effectively used as a troubleshooting aid in either of two ways. It can be used to locate electrical components by tracing hydraulic circuits through their respective flow control valves. The diagram can also be used to trace the hydraulic components in a given circuit.

Special mention was made of the symbol for the component enclosure. This symbol (usually a box drawn with a broken line) surrounds either a valve assembly or a group of valves and components in a common location. The component enclosure symbol indicates the location or physical grouping of the valves and components and is not indicating hydraulic lines or circuits.

When you are doing the initial troubleshooting on an inoperative hydraulic system, you will first need to determine if the malfunction is hydraulic in nature or is in the electrical control system.

When working with actual hydraulic equipment, it is important that you view the entire hydraulic design as an integrated system. Any modifications or repairs must be compatible with the system. In order to effectively maintain the system you must understand how it works and be aware of the various system pressures.

Understanding and practicing good safety procedures is mandatory in hydraulic work. You must be aware of the high pressures and the hazards encountered because of them.

Chapter Questions

Thinking through the text

1.   Draw and identify the hydraulic symbols for a pump, a two-way directional valve, a check valve, a blocked valve port, and a double-acting cylinder.

2. What is the difference between a direct- and a pilot-operated flow control valve? Why is the pilot-operated valve used?

3. Draw a component enclosure symbol. What does this symbol mean?

4. Draw the symbol and describe the purpose of each of the following lines: a working line, a pilot line, and a drain line.

5. What are the typical main line hydraulic pressures (rated in psi) mentioned in this chapter?

6. List two indications of hydraulic component failure. Give examples of each type of failure.

7. What specific hazards are mentioned as areas demanding attention when working on hydraulic systems?

Deepening your electrical understanding

8. Draw a simple working hydraulic diagram with a pump, a main pressure relief valve, a two-way valve, and a hydraulic cylinder. (You could modify the ejector cylinder circuit from Appendix B. Include pump PF2, valve 3 draining directly to the tank, valve 41, and the ejector cylinder.)

9. Draw three separate diagrams of a four-way valve with three envelopes ported (which means that they are "drilled") so that: (1) the center position is blocked, (2) a cylinder will extend in one control position, and (3) the cylinder will retract in the other position. In the first diagram, draw the lines through the left envelope to an extended cylinder. In the second diagram, draw the blocked lines. In the third diagram, draw the lines through the right envelope to a retracted cylinder.

10. Generally, when a hydraulic cylinder or motor malfunctions, a problem caused by an electrical control will show different characteristics than a problem caused by the hydraulic system. What are the characteristics of the two types of failures? Why do you think they act as they do?

Complete Electrical Diagram[1]

Electrical Diagram Legend

Selector Switches
S1   Operation
S2   Screw operation
S3   Mold open-close
S4   Plunger forward-return
S5   Screw unit forward-return
S6   Mold height adjust
S7   Mold height

Clamp Switches
SW3   Heater power
SW5   Control power
SW8   Press slow
SW9   Fast mold-close
SW10 Intrusion
SW12 Screw speed slow

Limit Switches
LS1   Mold open
LS2   Mold lock-up
LS3   Single cycle
LS5   Feed
LS6   Screw unit stroke
LS7   Slow down
LS8   Ejector forward
LS9   Ejector stroke
LS10 Rear gate safety
LS11 High pressure
LS12 Low pressure
LS14 Emergency mold-open
LS15 Ejector return
LS20 Lubrication

Push-Button Switches
PBM   Motor start
PBS   Motor stop
PBE   Ejector

---

[1] This diagram was supplied by Toyomenka (American), Inc., Cerritos, California. It is the electrical diagram of the Kawaguchi JEKS 180 plastic injection molding machine. The diagram shows the complete control circut but does not include the fused overloads, the motor circuit, the heater and thermocouple circuits, or other supplementary electrical information which might normally be shown on an electrical diagram.

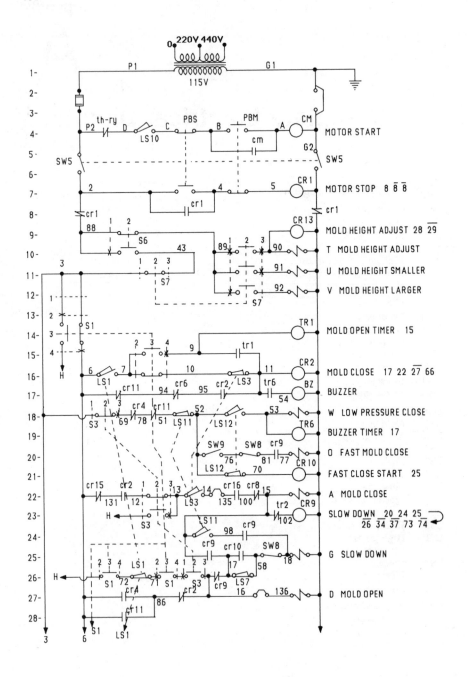

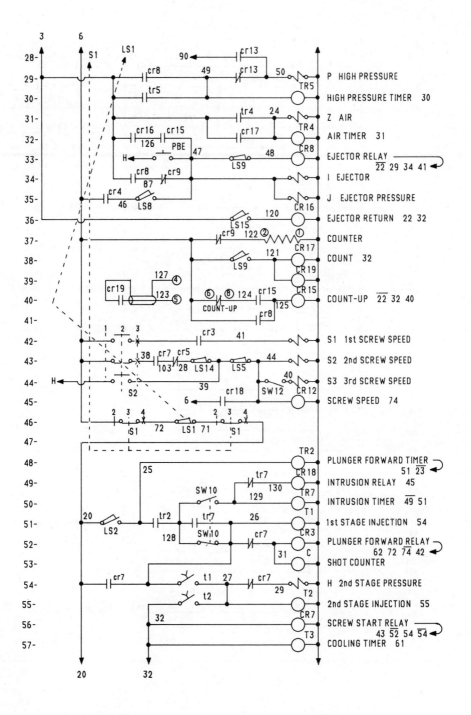

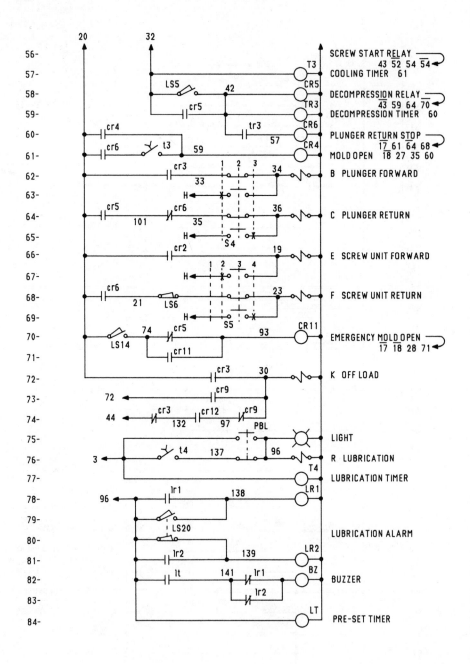

B

Complete Hydraulic Diagram[1]

[1] This diagram was supplied by Toyomenka (American), Inc., Cerritos, California. It is the hydraulic diagram of the Kawaguchi JEKS 180 plastic injection molding machine.

Mold Space Adjustment

Clamp Cylinder   Ejector Cylinder

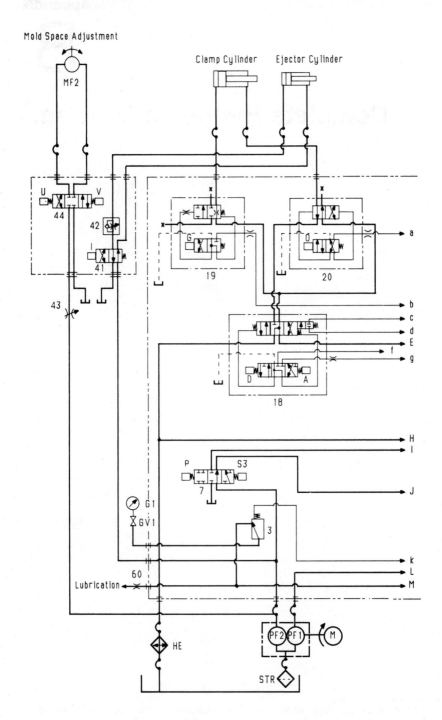

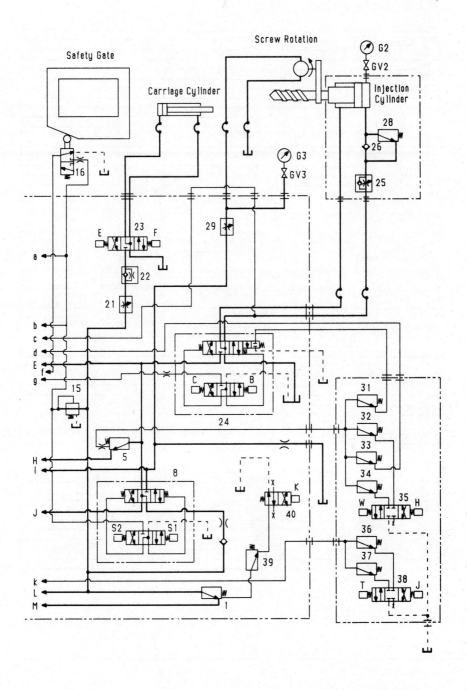

HYDRAULIC COMPONENTS			
M	MOTOR	22KW x 6P	
PF1	PUMP	21G SQP21-21-8-1BB-10	
PF2	PUMP	8G	
MF1	HYD. MOTOR	MIC-033	
MF2	HYD. MOTOR	H-170	
HE	HEAT EXCHANGER	FK-1604B	
STR	SUCTION STRAINER	PF-120	
G1	PRESSURE GAGE	BU-3/8 (3500 PSI)	MAIN PRESSURE
G2	PRESSURE GAGE	AU-3/8 (3500 PSI)	BACK PRESSURE
G3	PRESSURE GAGE	BU-3/8 (3500 PSI)	HYD. MOTOR
GV1	GAGE VALVE	GV-03-02	G1
GV2	GAGE VALVE	GV-03-02	G2
GV3	GAGE VALVE	GV-03-02	G3
1	RELIEF VALVE	BG-03-3233	SET AT 2000 PSI
3	RELIEF VALVE	BG-03-3233	SET AT 2000 PSI
5	RELIEF VALVE	BG-03-3233	SET AT 2000 PSI
7	SOLENOID VALVE	DSG-03-3C0-RQ115-4022	SOL-P KEEPS LINE PRESSURE
			SOL-S3 NO. 3 SCREW SPEED
8	SOL. PILOT VALVE	DSHG-06-3C5-E-R115	SOL-S1 NO. 1 SCREW SPEED
			SOL-S2 NO. 2 SCREW SPEED
13	ANGLE CHECK VALVE	CRG-06-5-3013	MINIMUM LINE PRESSURE
15	REDUCING VALVE	RG-03-B-2016	PILOT PRESSURE FOR SPOOL SHIFT
16	PILOT VALVE	SD-859-20	SHUT OFF FLOW TO VALVE NO 18
			WHEN SAFETY GATE IS OPEN
18	SOL. PILOT VALVE	DSHG-06-3C5-E-RG115	SOL-A MOLD CLOSE
			SOL-D MOLD OPEN
19	SOL. PILOT VALVE	DSHG-06-280-E-R2-RG115	SOL-G WHEN DE-ENERGIZED
			THROTTLES FLOW TO CLAMP CYLR
20	SOL. PILOT VALVE	DSHG-060280-E-R115	SOL-O FASTER MOLD CLOSE
21	FLOW CONTROL VALVE	FG-O1-8-N-1103	SPEED OF CARRIAGE CYLINDER
22	CHECK VALVE	SD-862-11	KEEP PRESSURE IN CARRIAGE CYLR
23	SOLENOID VALVE	DSG-01-3C40-A115-3123	CARRIAGE CYLINDER FWD/RTN
24	SOL. PILOT VALVE	DSHG-06-3C40-E-RG115	PLUNGER FWD/RTN
25	THROTTLE CHECK VALVE	SRC-06-4-4111	CONTROLS SPEED OF INJECTION
26	CHECK VALVE		STOPS INJECTION CYLINDER FLOW
28	RELIEF VALVE	BG-03-3221	BACK PRESSURE ADJUSTMENT
29	FLOW CONTROL VLV	FG-03-125-2110	SCREW SPEED
31	RELIEF VALVE	DG-01-22	1ST STAGE INJECTION PRESSURE
32	RELIEF VALVE	DG-01-22	2ND STAGE INJECTION PRESSURE
33	RELIEF VALVE	DG-01-22	CONTROLS LOCK UP PRESSURE
			MAX PRESSURE 16000 PSI
34	RELIEF VALVE	DG-01-22	LOW PRESSURE CLOSING
35	SOLENOID VALVE	DSG-01-3C2-A115-31	SOL-H 2ND STAGE PRESSURE
			SOL-W LOW PRESSURE CLOSING
36	RELIEF VALVE	DG-01-22	EJECTOR PRESSURE
37	RELIEF VALVE	DG-01-2216 (1100 PSI)	PRESSURE ON HYD. MOTOR
38	SOLENOID VALVE	DSG-01-3C2-A115-31	SOL-J EJECTOR PRESSURE
			SOL-T HYD. MOTOR PRESSURE
39	RELIEF VALVE	DG-01-2216 (1100 PSI)	
40	SOLENOID VALVE	DSG-01-2B2-A115-31	SOL-K HIGH PRESSURE ON P1 PUMP
41	SOLENOID VALVE	DSG-03-2B3-RQ115-4025	SOL-I EJECTOR FWD
42	THROTTLE CK VALVE	SRCG-06-H-4111	EJECTOR SPEED
43	NEEDLE VALVE	GCTR-02-3107	MOLD HEIGHT ADJUST SPEED
44	SOLENOID VALVE	DSG-01-3C2-A115-31	HYD. MOTOR TURNING DIRECTION
60	THROTTLE VALVE	SNS-385	

Useful Electrical Formulas

To find:	Single-phase ac	Three-phase ac
Kilowatts (kW)	$\dfrac{E \times I \times PF}{1,000}$	$\dfrac{E \times I \times PF \times 1.73}{1,000}$
Kilovoltamperes (kVA)	$\dfrac{E \times I}{1,000}$	$\dfrac{E \times I \times 1.73}{1,000}$
Amperes when kW is known	$\dfrac{kW \times 1,000}{E \times PF}$	$\dfrac{kW \times 1,000}{E \times PF \times 1.73}$
Amperes when HP is known	$\dfrac{HP \times 746}{E \times \%eff \times PF}$	$\dfrac{HP \times 746}{E \times \%eff \times PF \times 1.73}$
Amperes when kVA is known	$\dfrac{kVA \times 1,000}{E}$	$\dfrac{kVA \times 1,000}{E \times 1.73}$
Horsepower (HP)	$\dfrac{E \times I \times \%eff \times PF}{746}$	$\dfrac{E \times I \times \%eff \times PF \times 1.73}{746}$

NOTE: $\%eff$ = percent efficiency = $\dfrac{output}{input}$

E = electromotive force in volts
I = current in amperes
R = resistance in ohms
HP = horsepower (1 hp = 746 W)
Three-phase current = 1.73 × single-phase current

PF = power factor = $\dfrac{power\ used}{apparent\ power}$ = $\dfrac{kW}{kVA}$

Useful Circuit Diagrams[1]

---

[1] All drawings with the exception of the three-phase motor windings and connections have been provided through the courtesy of Furnas Electric Company, Batavia, Illinois.

Control Circuit Diagrams

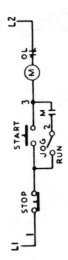

Fig. 1. Three Wire Control Giving Low Voltage Protection Single Two Button Pushbutton Station

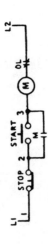

Fig. 2. Three Wire Control Giving Low Voltage Protection Multiple Two Button Pushbutton Stations

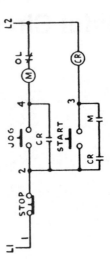

Fig. 3. Three Wire Control Giving Low Voltage Protection with Safe-Run Selector Switch

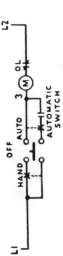

Fig. 4. Three Wire Control for Jog or Run Using Start-Stop Pushbuttons and Jog-Run Selector Switch

Fig. 5. Control for Jogging-Start-Stop All with Pushbuttons

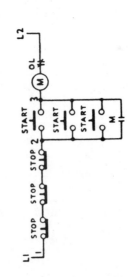

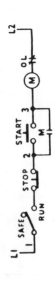

Fig. 6. Two Wire Control Giving Low Voltage Release Only Using **Hand-Off-Auto** Selector Switch

204

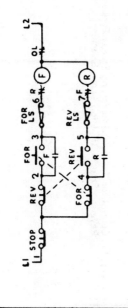

Fig. 7. Two Wire Control for Reversing Jogging. Using Single Two Button Pushbutton Station

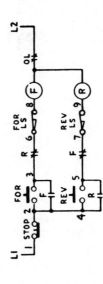

Fig. 8. Three Wire Control for Instant Reversing Applications Using Single Three Button Pushbutton Station

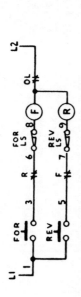

Fig. 9. Three Wire Control for Reversing Using Single Three Button Pushbutton Station

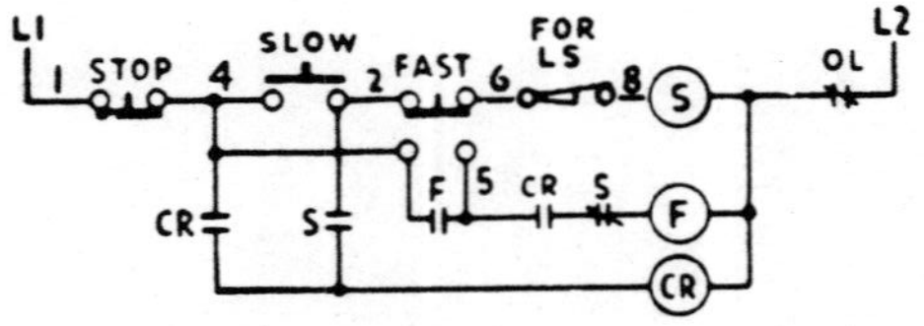

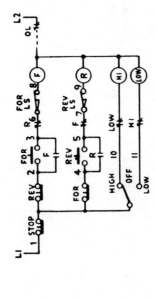

Fig. 11. Control for Two Speed Reversing Starter Forward, Reverse, Stop, with High, Low Selector Switch

Fig. 10. Control for Two Speed with a Compelling Relay to Insure Starting on Slow Speed

Three-Phase AC Motor Windings and Connections

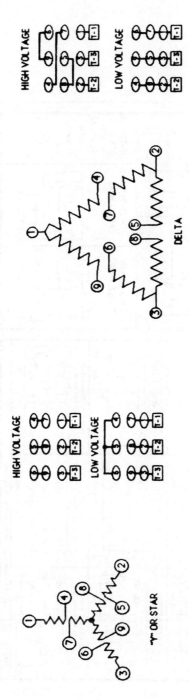

Drum Controller Connection Diagrams

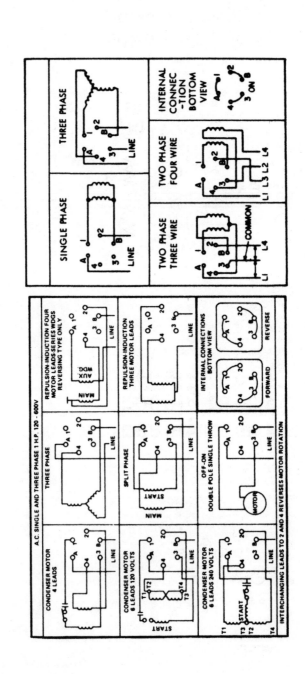

Hydraulic Troubleshooting Guide[1]

[1] This material is used by permission of Nickerson Machinery Co., Accord, Massachusetts. It is taken from their 1986 supply catalog pages 209 to 211.

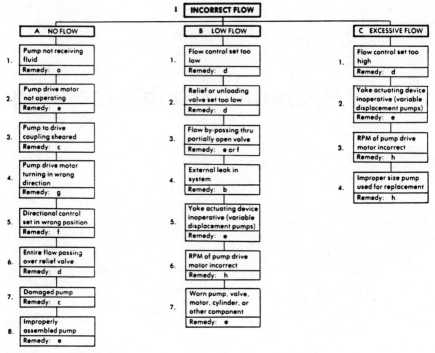

I | INCORRECT FLOW

A   NO FLOW

1. Pump not receiving fluid
   Remedy: a

2. Pump drive motor not operating
   Remedy: e

3. Pump to drive coupling sheared
   Remedy: c

4. Pump drive motor turning in wrong direction
   Remedy: g

5. Directional control set in wrong position
   Remedy: f

6. Entire flow passing over relief valve
   Remedy: d

7. Damaged pump
   Remedy: c

8. Improperly assembled pump
   Remedy: e

B   LOW FLOW

1. Flow control set too low
   Remedy: d

2. Relief or unloading valve set too low
   Remedy: d

3. Flow by-passing thru partially open valve
   Remedy: e or f

4. External leak in system
   Remedy: b

5. Yoke actuating device inoperative (variable displacement pumps)
   Remedy: e

6. RPM of pump drive motor incorrect
   Remedy: h

7. Worn pump, valve, motor, cylinder, or other component
   Remedy: e

C   EXCESSIVE FLOW

1. Flow control set too high
   Remedy: d

2. Yoke actuating device inoperative (variable displacement pumps)
   Remedy: e

3. RPM of pump drive motor incorrect
   Remedy: h

4. Improper size pump used for replacement
   Remedy: h

REMEDIES:

a. Any or all of the following: Replace dirty filters - clean clogged inlet line - Clean reservoir breather vent - Fill reservoir to proper level - Overhaul or replace supercharge pump.

b. Tighten leaky connections - Bleed air from system.

c. Check for damaged pump or pump drive - replace and align coupling.

d. Adjust

e. Overhaul or replace.

f. Check position of manually operated controls - Check electrical circuit on solenoid operated controls - Repair or replace pilot pressure pump.

g. Reverse rotation.

h. Replace with correct unit.

II EXCESSIVE NOISE

	A PUMP NOISY				B MOTOR NOISY		C RELIEF VALVE NOISY
1.	Cavitation / Remedy: a	3.	Coupling Mis-aligned / Remedy: c	1.	Coupling Mis-aligned / Remedy: c	1.	Setting too low or too close to another valve setting / Remedy: d
2.	Air in Fluid / Remedy: b	4.	Pump Worn or Damaged / Remedy: e	2.	Motor or Coupling Worn or Damaged / Remedy: e	2.	Worn poppet and seat / Remedy: e

REMEDIES:

a. Any or all of the following: Replace dirty-filters — Wash strainers in solvent compatible with system fluid — Clean clogged inlet line — Clean reservoir breather vent — Change system fluid — Change to proper pump drive motor speed — Overhaul or replace supercharge pump — Fluid may be too cold

b. Any or all of the following: Tighten leaky inlet connections —

Fill reservoir to proper level (with rare exception all return lines should be below fluid level in reservoir) — Bleed air from system — Replace pump shaft seal (and shaft if worn at seal journal)

c. Align unit and check condition of seals, bearings and coupling

d. Install pressure gauge and adjust to correct pressure

e. Overhaul or replace

III EXCESSIVE HEAT

	A PUMP HEATED		B MOTOR HEATED		C RELIEF VALVE HEATED		D FLUID HEATED
1.	Fluid heated / Remedy: See column D	1.	Fluid heated / Remedy: See column D	1.	Fluid heated / Remedy: See column D	1.	System pressure too high / Remedy: d
2.	Cavitation / Remedy: a	2.	Relief or unloading valve set too high / Remedy: d	2.	Valve setting incorrect / Remedy: d	2.	Unloading valve set too high / Remedy: d
3.	Air in fluid / Remedy: b	3.	Excessive load / Remedy: c	3.	Worn or damaged valve / Remedy: e	3.	Fluid dirty or low supply / Remedy: f
4.	Relief or unloading valve set too high / Remedy: d	4.	Worn or damaged motor / Remedy: e			4.	Incorrect fluid viscosity / Remedy: f
5.	Excessive load / Remedy: c					5.	Faulty fluid cooling system / Remedy: g
6.	Worn or damaged pump / Remedy: e					6.	Worn pump, valve, motor, cylinder or other component / Remedy: e

REMEDIES:

a. Any or all of the following: Replace dirty filters · Clean clogged inlet line · Clean reservoir breather vent · Change system fluid · Change to proper pump drive motor speed · Overhaul or replace supercharge pump.

b. Any or all of the following: Tighten leaky inlet connections · Fill reservoir to proper level (with rare exception all return lines should be below fluid level in reservoir) · Bleed air from system · Replace pump shaft seal (and shaft if worn at seal journal).

c. Align unit and check condition of seals and bearings · Locate and correct mechanical binding · Check for work load in excess of circuit design.

d. Install pressure gauge and adjust to correct pressure (Keep at least 125 PSI difference between valve settings).

e. Overhaul or replace.

f. Change filters and also system fluid if of improper viscosity · Fill reservoir to proper level.

g. Clean cooler and/or cooler strainer · Replace cooler control valve · Repair or replace cooler.

IV INCORRECT PRESSURE

A NO PRESSURE	B LOW PRESSURE	C ERRATIC PRESSURE	D EXCESSIVE PRESSURE
1. No flow — Remedy: See Chart I, column A	1. Pressure relief path exists — Remedy: See Chart I, column A and B	1. Air in fluid — Remedy: b	1. Pressure reducing, relief or unloading valve misadjusted — Remedy: d
	2. Pressure reducing valve set too low — Remedy: d	2. Worn relief valve — Remedy: e	2. Yoke actuating device inoperative (variable displacement pumps) — Remedy: e
	3. Pressure reducing valve damaged — Remedy: e	3. Contamination in fluid — Remedy: a	3. Pressure reducing, relief or unloading valve worn or damaged — Remedy: e
	4. Damaged pump, motor or cylinder — Remedy: e	4. Accumulator defective or has lost charge — Remedy: c	
		5. Worn pump, motor or cylinder — Remedy: e	

REMEDIES:
a. Replace dirty filters and system fluid.
b. Tighten leaky connections (fill reservoir to proper level and bleed air from system)
c. Check gas valve for leakage · Change to correct pressure · Overhaul if defective.
d. Adjust
e. Overhaul or replace.

V FAULTY OPERATION

A NO MOVEMENT	B SLOW MOVEMENT	C ERRATIC MOVEMENT	D EXCESSIVE SPEED OR MOVEMENT
1. No flow or or pressure — Remedy: See Chart I	1. Low flow — Remedy: See Chart I	1. Erratic pressure — Remedy: See Chart IV	1. Excessive flow — Remedy: See Chart I
2. Limit or sequence device (mechanical, electrical, or hydraulic) inoperative or midadjusted — Remedy: e	2. Fluid viscosity too high — Remedy: a	2. Air in fluid — Remedy: See Chart II	2. Feedback transducer malfunctioning — Remedy: e
3. Mechanical bind — Remedy: b	3. Insufficient control pressure for valves — Remedy: See Chart IV	3. No lubrication of machine ways or linkage — Remedy: g	3. Misadjusted or malfunctioning servo amplifier — Remedy: c
4. No command signal to servo amplifier — Remedy: f	4. No lubrication of machine ways or linkage — Remedy: g	4. Erratic command signal — Remedy: f	4. Over-riding work load — Remedy: h
5. Inoperative or mis-adjusted servo amplifier — Remedy: c	5. Misadjusted or malfunctioning servo amplifier — Remedy: c	5. Misadjusted or malfunctioning servo amplifier — Remedy: c	
6. Inoperative servo valve — Remedy: e	6. Sticking servo valve — Remedy: d	6. Malfunctioning feedback transducer — Remedy: e	
7. Worn or damaged cylinder or motor — Remedy: e	7. Worn or damaged cylinder or motor — Remedy: e	7. Sticking servo valve — Remedy: d	
		8. Worn or damaged cylinder or motor — Remedy: e	

REMEDIES:
a. Fluid may be too cold or should be changed to clean fluid of correct viscosity
b. Locate bind and repair
c. Adjust, repair, or replace
d. Clean and adjust or replace — Check condition of system fluid and filters
e. Overhaul or replace
f. Repair command console or interconnecting wires
g. Lubricate
h. Adjust, repair, or replace counterbalance valve.

Instrument Suppliers

The following suppliers are those whose instruments were described in the text:

Greenlee BEHA Corporation
  4455 Boeing Drive
  Rockford, IL 61109
  (800) 435-0786
Hioki-RCC, Inc.
  198 Route 206
  South Somerville, NJ 08876
  (201) 874-6484
A. W. Sperry Instruments, Inc.
  245 Marcus Blvd.
  Hauppauge, NY 11788
  (800) 645-5398
TIF Instruments, Inc.
  9101 NW 7th Ave.
  Miami, FL 33150
  (305) 757-8811

ADDENDUM: The Greenlee BEHA UNITEST 600 replaces the UNITEST 575 referred to in the text.

Index

About the Author

Lynn Lundquist is a veteran troubleshooter and licensed electrician. He has been the general maintenance manager in plastic injection molding and die casting shops for eight years. In addition, he is an experienced machinist, welder, and metal fabricator. He has designed and built automated equipment, and holds five issued U.S. patents. Mr. Lundquist has both a B.A. and a Master's degree in education.